THE COMMUNITY ORCHESTRA

THE COMMUNITY ORCHESTRA

A Handbook for
Conductors, Managers, and
Boards

JAMES VAN HORN

GREENWOOD PRESS
WESTPORT, CONNECTICUT•LONDON, ENGLAND

Library of Congress Cataloging in Publication Data

Van Horn, James.
    The community orchestra.

    Bibliography: p.
    Includes index.
    1. Conducting. 2. Orchestra. 3. Community music.
4. Music--Economic aspects. I. Title
MT85.V27   785'.06'607   78-60531
ISBN 0-313-20562-0

Library of Congress Catalog Card Number: 78-60531
ISBN: 0-313-20562-0

First published in 1979

Greenwood Press, Inc.
51 Riverside Avenue, Westport, Connecticut 06880

Printed in the United States of America

10 9 8 7 6 5 4 3 2 1

Dedicated to the memory of
HELEN M. THOMPSON
who helped so much

Contents

Preface

Symphony orchestras are more than music; they are music plus excellent organization. The author's fifteen years' experience as conductor of the Port Angeles, Washington, Symphony together with working with other community groups for years have convinced him that no matter how talented the conductor or how enthusiastic the audience, flabby organization is, at best, counterproductive.

The guidelines in this book are addressed specifically to those conductors and orchestras that must function without benefit of professional managerial assistance, at least in their formative years. Many of the procedures outlined in this book are conducive to good human relations, efficiency, and artistic effectiveness which can be of great help to younger conductors especially, for they are the ones who are most often called upon to work with orchestras with minimal or no managerial help.

While the American Symphony Orchestra League has published handbooks for several different phases of orchestral operations, there is nothing published of specific benefit for the conductors of smaller, more isolated orchestras.

The basic conducting texts (Rudolf, Boult, McElheran, Scherchen, and others) limit themselves to the problems of attaining a workable conducting technique but do not deal with any of the special problems pertaining to the myriad details which are necessary in effecting the total operation of community orchestras, particularly where no trained managerial help is available. McElheran moves closer to some of these problems than other texts, but he limits himself to the more obvious items such as selecting proper podium height.

This guide is the result of the author's many years as a community orchestra conductor-manager-stagehand-promotion department-fund raiser. It is designed to be an orderly list of priorities which, if followed, will help the newcomer to an orchestra avoid many of the pitfalls which have so often plagued community orchestras and their conductors. It is not offered as a guarantee of success, but only as a helpful guide.

To begin with, we must consider operational activities: the community orchestra as an organization (Chapter 1), community relations (Chapter 2), and the actual day-to-day mechanics of keeping an orchestra running (Chapter 3). While the advice given here is aimed mainly at conductors, others involved with community orchestras, such as orchestra boards and women's committees, may also benefit from some of the suggestions. Furthermore, some of the principles will transfer quite well to other organizations such as the community chorus or band or opera group.

It is the young conductor, perhaps assuming a first position of responsibility in a community remote from metropolitan centers, who is most in need of guidelines regarding effective operational procedures. On the other hand, where the community orchestra coexists within a metropolitan area as a complement or supplement to an established professional symphony orchestra, some revisions of the suggestions given here may be in order. Just as when one purchases a set of house-plans through a magazine advertisement, changes must be made to suit the topography of the building site, so the suggestions given here may have to be altered to suit local conditions.

Chapters 4 (Conducting as Art and Craft) and 5 (Some Rehearsal Procedures) are devoted to some consideration of the training of community orchestra conductors as well as to other strictly musical aspects of the conductor's task: auditioning players, and rehearsal procedures and techniques. Some ideas in these two chapters may well be of interest to boards and women's associations as well.

The final three chapters, devoted to programming considerations, are designed to help the fledgling conductor with the kind of commonsense wisdom that more mature conductors will already have gained through experience. All too often a young conductor with a master's or doctor's degree comes into the community orchestra with a natural desire to "cut a wide swath" in programming. Considering the vastness of the orchestral repertoire, the problem of programming seems largely a matter of "what works can I play?" when actually successful programming is more likely to depend upon the decision, "what works must I avoid?"

Portions of Chapter 8 are the result of a limited survey of community orchestra programs together with analysis of the more comprehensive surveys published by Broadcast Music, Inc. (BMI) and Kate Hevner Mueller.*

Conductors must learn to deal with real or imagined pressures which are applied concerning program selection. Does such pressure actually exist, or are conductors basically fearful that it might happen? These questions are raised most often in the matter of programming contemporary music. Some answers to these and other questions of programming are posed in Chapter 8. We trust that this guide, then, can be of help to the novice conductor in his first years with a community orchestra.

Many persons have contributed generously to this study: conductors, managers, publishers, and orchestral players. Special thanks must be extended to the Board of Directors and players of the Port Angeles Symphony Orchestra, who, for fifteen years, allowed the author to make music with them as their conductor. Many of the faculty members of the University of Washington School of Music have offered valuable suggestions and have provided much encouragement. Most especially, the author wishes to thank Professor Demar Irvine who encouraged publication of this guide and offered invaluable assistance in the actual writing, members of the Philadelphia String Quartet, the Soni Ventorum Woodwind Quintet, and members of the instrumental faculty of the University of Washington School of Music who generously contributed suggestions concerning repertoire for player auditions.

To both Professor Samuel Krachmalnick and Dr. Stanley Chapple, past Directors of Symphony and Opera at the University of Washington, hearty thanks for much encouragement both in the preparation of this guide and for many helpful suggestions contained herein not always properly acknowledged otherwise.

Mr. Richard Wangerin, former president of the American Symphony Orchestra League, and his office staff circulated my own questionnaire to a number of community orchestra conductors. Without that assistance, the questionnaire could not have been circulated so efficiently.

The author wishes to thank McGraw-Hill Book Company for their gracious permission to use the quotation from Carl Bamberger's book, *The Conductor's Art*, and the American Symphony Orchestra League for permission to use the extensive quotations from various pamphlets and articles by the late Helen M. Thompson.

---

*James G. Roy, Jr., ed., *BMI Orchestral Program Survey, 1969–70 Concert Season* (New York: Broadcast Music, Inc., 1970) and Kate Hevner Mueller, *Twenty-seven Major American Symphony Orchestras: A History and Analysis of Their Repertoires, Seasons 1942–43 through 1969–70* (Bloomington, Indiana: Indiana University Press, 1973).

   Two members of my own family contributed much to this guide. My father did not live to see its completion, but his life was governed by the maxim of completing any task once undertaken; thus, once begun, this guide had to be finished—he would have wanted it that way. My wife, Joanne, has endured much during the writing. Without her faithful encouragement, its completion would have been far more arduous.

                                                            James Van Horn

THE COMMUNITY ORCHESTRA

chapter 1

The Community Orchestra as an Organization

Our first consideration is to examine the kind of structure suitable for community symphony orchestras in relative isolation from larger metropolitan centers. Such orchestras serve self-sufficient cultural areas, contributing to community-wide needs. This contrasts with the so-called community orchestra *within* large metropolitan areas, where professional organizations bear the main cultural load, and subsidiary organizations represent added music-making, serving special segments of the population, or even providing satisfaction and fulfillment for the players themselves.

Where the orchestra exists only as an outlet for the players, the organizational structure can be quite casual. A committee to take care of the orchestra's routine business, plus suitable arrangements for any desired social functions, will usually suffice.

What we shall outline below in regard to the first type of community orchestra is merely a skeleton of the total orchestral organizational structure. This outline is purposely not filled in since it is much easier to begin with a simple organizational scheme to fill in additional committees and positions as the needs arise. The late Mrs. Helen M. Thompson, formerly executive vice-president of the American Symphony Orchestra League and later manager of the New York Philharmonic Orchestra, stated it very clearly: "Many orchestras prefer to adopt as simple a constitution and as few by-laws as possible, thereby establishing a flexible legal instrument which permits ready adjustment of operations to the conditions obtaining at any time. Generally speaking this seems to be a practical procedure."[1]

In all cases, the structure must be highly flexible. A rigid structure fetters the organization so that growth or change of direction becomes far more difficult to accomplish. An orchestra financed solely from the dues of the playing members, plus receipts from a free-will collection at intermission, will not need a finance committee to raise funds until such time as the orchestra decides that such a policy is desirable for the sake of proper growth and nourishment. The only thing necessary in such a case is that the organizing document allow for additional committees and personnel to be added at such time as they are deemed necessary.

The first order of any orchestra's business is the making of music. To do that effectively, the mind must be freed from the provocations and irritations of more mundane, routine, practical matters. The artistic goals must be backed up by a smoothly functioning organization. It is therefore relevant to consider organizational questions first. The conductor has primary responsibility for the success of the community orchestra, but the weight of responsibility is shared by the working organization behind the conductor—that part of the iceberg that remains hidden from casual view. The organizational structure will typically include a Board of Directors, a women's association, and some kind of managerial assistance—paid or volunteer.

Ideally, the community orchestra will have a trained manager whose duties include the supervision of all the details of the orchestra's business: ticket sales, rehearsal and concert arrangements, and anything else which needs doing. The manager is really responsible for everything except conducting the orchestra and playing the instruments. Mrs. Thompson has whimsically but realistically summed up the duties of the manager as follows:

> It's up to him to see that the stage hands are sober, that the conductor has a baton, that the librarian has the music in order, that the musicians arrive at rehearsals on time and at concerts in the proper attire, that the women's committee and the executive board do their jobs, that the programs are printed *and* delivered, that the tympani heads are not cracked, that those to be photographed and those doing the photographing arrive at the same place at the same time, that the bills are paid, that the concert hall is neither too cold nor too hot, that soloists are met at trains, that something new and different happens constantly, that the orchestra is progressing in every way, that everyone is kept happy as much of the time as possible and that he himself lives long enough to record the whole proceedings for posterity.[2]

By performing these important chores, the manager frees the time and energies of the conductor for musical duties. For smaller groups without such managerial assistance, it is a fact of life that much of the conductor's energy is drained away on organizational matters. At the beginning of an orchestra's life, it may be the conductor who must assume the manager's duties; but, as Mrs. Thompson pointed out to the author in 1959, he should rid himself of managerial functions as soon as possible. The orchestra cannot properly function musically if the conductor spends most of his time on things non-musical.

BOARD OF DIRECTORS

The first and most important organizational step is to form a Board of Directors to attend to the business and legal matters of the orchestra. The Board is the legal entity; once formed, its first order of business should be to incorporate the orchestra under whatever nonprofit cultural and educational statutes obtain in the particular state of incorporation. The act of incorporation gives the orchestra a *legal* identity, one which is very important considering that the engaging of soloists, rental of music, rental of rehearsal and performing spaces, and a myriad of other details involves the signing of contracts which are binding on the signing parties. It is better if these contracts are binding on a corporation, including the nonprofit kind, than on a single individual. That person would be the conductor and generally his position, particularly at the outset, is precarious enough without his becoming involved in contractual matters. To quote Mrs. Thompson once more:

> A Corporation may owe money, but the incorporators as individuals are under no obligation to pay the debt. As a corporation, all of the orchestra's business relations are facilitated. Contracts with conductors, musicians, soloists, and business houses are made definite and certain. Business relations with banking institutions are facilitated—a very important point when the organization is forced to borrow money for emergencies.
>
> The act of incorporating insures a desired continuity, for rights and duties descend to the successive officers of a corporation. A corporation cannot be dissolved except by definite procedures prescribed by law. Furthermore, a corporation may receive certain tax advantages not available to associations.[3]

Equally important is that for a nonprofit corporation contributions to the orchestra can become tax deductions for the donors under certain conditions, and the corporation can be exempt from corporate income taxes. These conditions are delineated by the United States Bureau of Internal Revenue and are summarized in Appendix A at the end of this guide. Of particular importance are the paragraphs on dissolution of such organizations.

A third factor in favor of incorporation is that certain grants are available to community orchestras. This is becoming more and more important in orchestra funding, particularly since the United States Congress has funded the National Endowment for the Arts. Such grants are available to organizations able to perform certain artistic functions, as special concerts, services to disadvantaged children, programs for minorities, and the like.

In many instances it will be the conductor who forms the orchestra in the first place, and who should take the initiative in securing a Board of Directors. Who should constitute the board? Experience has shown that a board may be made up of either people with a wide variety of interests and backgrounds or a close group of music lovers, often orchestra members themselves. However, most often a community-wide representation is able to function more effectively. In a letter to the present writer some years ago, Mrs. Thompson wrote: "Symphony orchestra musicians are wonderful people, but they are not the best fund raisers." Since one of the never-ending functions of the board is to raise money, Mrs. Thompson's advice is well taken. This is not to say that the orchestra members, particularly of a community orchestra, should not have voting representation on the board, but the balance of the board's makeup should draw on much wider community representation.

There is no ideal composition for an orchestra's Board of Directors. The conductor might begin by asking some of the orchestra members provide names of potentially interested community people. While it is not always necessary to use only community *leaders*, a few such persons are a real help in enlisting the aid of others.

As an example, the composition of the first Board of Directors of the Port Angeles Symphony, in the state of Washington, included several members of the orchestra together with the wife of the publisher of the local newspaper, three executives of local industries, the wife of the mayor, one of the leading physicians of the community, the wife of an influential clergyman, and others. Although many years have intervened, the composition of that orchestra's board remains relatively the same as at the outset, but with wider community representation.

What is needed, whether the board is composed of five or twenty-five members, is some representation from the schools, the media, the churches, and the professional community, plus a willing lawyer. The reason for legal representation is twofold: the attorney can be helpful in the preparation of the legal documents for incorporation, and he can read over any contracts that must be signed to make sure there are no problems in the fine print. Attorneys are usually willing to donate their services.

It must be assumed that with either a new board or a new conductor, the responsibilities of each will be clearly delineated. Even with a newly formed orchestra and board, there must be clearly stated goals which the board sets for the orchestra. The board must take the leadership role. It then serves as a set of ground rules with which the conductor can work. It is important early in the relationship between conductor and board that the total contribution of the conductor be spelled out. Where there is no paid management, often the conductor must assume more of the managerial duties, but this should be clearly understood and even made part of any contract between board and conductor.

It must also be assumed that the conductor will provide his own input to the board in matters pertaining to the orchestra's growth and direction. The conductor is the "expert," and any board which does not pay heed to his input is not utilizing him in the most efficient way. In the event the board takes a position which the conductor feels is not in the best interests of the orchestra, it is his moral obligation to voice his objections in the strongest possible terms. To do less, to sit idle watching such happen, would compromise his musical integrity.

Once the board is formed—and it is generally better to begin with fewer board members and gradually expand as the need arises—one of the first steps in the organizational procedure is to apply for membership in the American Symphony Orchestra League. This organization, chartered in 1942, is a mutual aid society for symphony orchestras, large and small, throughout the United States and Canada.

In the 1960s, there seemed to be a general movement of League officials away from the problems of the smaller orchestras; concern over this concentration on the specific problems of the major and metropolitan orchestras was voiced privately by many representatives from smaller orchestras. It cannot be denied that the larger orchestras needed much help in areas of funding (with many orchestras moving toward fifty-two-week seasons), foundations, and governmental legislation in the arts. More heartening is the news in the prospectus for the National Conference of 1974 that additional attention is being given the smaller orchestras.

The League's institution of five regional workshops has greatly expanded the assistance to smaller orchestras. In addition, the League has instituted some in-field consulting teams which are available to any member orchestra. Ralph Black, executive director of the League, has increased his own visits and during one four-day period visited some six Pacific Northwest orchestras, addressing groups at luncheons, dinners, board meetings, and rehearsals.

Black has the enthusiasm for symphony orchestras large and small equal to that of a tent-meeting evangelist and is always willing to speak. The only financial investment he requires of the orchestra is travel and hospitality.

Two other recent innovations are the formation of state or regional orchestra associations and the establishment of the Community-Urban Symphony Orchestra division (CUSO) under the umbrella of the League. The state associations offer all kinds of services: workshops, residencies, regional libraries, etc.

The American Symphony Orchestra League can be helpful to orchestras in many other ways, some of which will be mentioned in the course of this study. For example, the League provides an important service by publishing various handbooks. A new board should secure immediately two of these from the League office: *Report of Study on Governing Boards of Symphony Orchestras* and *A Study of Symphony Orchestra Legal Documents.*[4] Perusal of these volumes will help a board avoid many of the problems which might otherwise develop.

The structure of the board will vary from community to community. Generally, the incorporation procedure will require at least three officers who will typically form the executive committee. Some standing committees will be needed to which various functions can be delegated so that the entire board need not meet as a committee of the whole discussing each and every phase of the orchestra's life.

Some orchestras have found it helpful to have a music advisory committee to assist the conductor in planning programs, engaging soloists, and other musical matters. While some conductors are receptive to this and others are not, in either case it is well for the conductor to bear in mind: a music advisory committee, having approved a season's programs, is less vulnerable to criticism of the programming than would be the conductor who has to bear the sole responsibility. A sympathetic committee can often help the conductor avoid programming problems which detract from the orchestra's usefulness.

A budget and/or finance committee is a necessity. It devolves upon this committee to plan a workable budget that can be submitted to the entire board for approval. A few people can plan a budget far more effectively than a large group. Budgets are very often altered during the discussion by the whole board, but it consumes less time of busy people to have an independent committee prepare the budget for discussion.

Many orchestras include committees on ticket sales, special fundraising projects, capital contributions, and the like. This must, of necessity, vary with the needs of the orchestra and the people who comprise the board.

In some larger orchestras, membership on the Board of Directors is almost an honorary appointment, sometimes coincident with the size of an individual's contribution. But in many of these cases, the orchestra functions with a paid manager and office staff who look after the day-to-day routine of business.

A word of caution: much of the detail of board structure should be a part of the by-laws rather than the constitution. As needs change, it is easier to change the by-laws than to alter the constitution. In some states, organizations chartered by the state have far more legal difficulties in amending constitutions than in changing by-laws.

It behooves an orchestra to be very careful in the selection of board members. A portrait of the ideal board member, (and again the author is indebted to Ralph Black) is of a leader, dedicated to the orchestra, with boundless enthusiasm, who is a hard worker, dependable, a concert goer, and above all, a giver. It might be well to consider that if a board member is unwilling to give the orchestra of his or her time, talents, and *treasures*, it might be the time to consider replacing that person. An orchestra board needs people with all of these attributes. Anything less will cause problems in the end.

In summary, the board should be formed with as wide a base of community representation as possible; the board should incorporate the orchestra for the sake of legalities and more favorable fund-raising arguments; the orchestra should become a member of the American Symphony Orchestra League as soon as is practical; and the organization of the board should be as flexible as possible.

WOMEN'S COMMITTEE

A valuable help for a community orchestra is its Women's Committee (or Auxiliary, League or other such designation). In many orchestras, this group of dedicated women often performs more valuable service for the orchestra than the board or any other adjunct group which an orchestra has.

A five or ten year collection of official minutes of a community symphony orchestra's executive board meetings usually contains several familiar refrains—rather like the chorus of a song. . . . And each year's entries almost invariably include a graciously worded resolution commending "the ladies" on their excellent work on behalf of the orchestra and especially for their splendid efforts during the money-raising campaign.[5]

Care should be taken to insure that whatever projects are contemplated will be those that will realize a proper return on the investment of precious volunteer labor. A garage sale which returns only a few dollars is hardly worth the effort of the many volunteers who are willing to give time to the orchestra.

A quick perusal of the summary of fund-raising projects by women's associations of various orchestras published annually by the American Symphony Orchestra League (see Bibliography) will be helpful in determining what kinds of projects should be undertaken.

Many orchestras rely on their women's group to spearhead the sale of season tickets, as well as many other varied fund-raising ventures. The kinds of money-raising schemes which these groups promote are as varied as the communities in which they are found: balls, home tours, rummage sales, art auctions, magazine subscription campaigns, and fashion shows are among the promotions which these groups sponsor, often at handsome profits.

To be sure, many of these groups stress social activities and to a lesser extent some social exclusiveness. However, this seems to be truer of the established orchestras in large metropolitan areas. In the more geographically isolated orchestras, the women's association is a very strong and vital part of the total artistic community.

The American Symphony Orchestra League provides much assistance to women's committees. Various publications from the League office can be highly valuable not only in terms of helping organize a new group, but for strengthening an existing committee or association.

A women's committee can be further strengthened by having at least one of the group attend the League's annual conference, held each June. This conference is for members of women's committees, board members, managers, and conductors, but the various workshops for the women seem to be the highlight of each conference.

The conductor must not neglect his relationship with the women's committee, considering its importance to the orchestra. There are many ways in which the conductor can serve the group, including preconcert discussion of the music or talks to the group on other musical topics, as well as just stimulating interest in the orchestra. The conductor is a musical leader in his community and his presence at women's committee functions, when invited, can stimulate the growth and activities of the committee.

There are other ways in which members of the committee can be of help to the orchestra besides fund-raising. For social events, such as refreshment hours for orchestra players after rehearsals and concerts, or for a visiting soloist, the women's committee can be relied upon. At times when the orchestra budget is slim, office help can be a very expensive necessity which can be reduced by calling on the women's committee for volunteer typists, clerks, and other help in preparing bulk mailings or other routine chores that need to be done.

Women move about in a community; when their enthusiasm is aroused on behalf of any worthwhile cause, additional support comes with it. Enthusiasm is contagious; the women's association serves as a leavening agent for the rest of the community, which is more likely to be attracted to a bandwagon that already has a respectable following.

The organizational structure of the women's committee may be quite formal, with standing committees in charge of various projects, or less structured; but its relation to the orchestra's Board of Directors should be a close one.* Many orchestras have one or more of the women's committee serving as voting board members. This is more particularly true in smaller cities, but can be of advantage in larger ones as well. It is very important that each group know what the other is doing so that all activities may be coordinated.

In some orchestras, the women's committee sponsors scholarships for deserving young musicians, sponsors recitals and appearances of young soloists with the orchestras, and is able to contribute greatly to the overall musical strength of the community. Such support for younger musicians helps insure a future supply of players for the orchestra.

In summary, any orchestra, old or newly founded, needs its women's committee.

> For the "top brass" notwithstanding, it is usually "the ladies" who do the street pounding and telephoning in order to actually sell symphony tickets. It is they who do the year-in, year-out word-of-mouth symphony promotion, and therein lies the basic story of the success of many community symphonies.[6]

These dedicated women can serve in many ways: ticket sales, fund-raising, promoting the orchestra, encouraging young musicians, and helping with many of the routine business tasks for which many smaller orchestras cannot afford to pay secretarial help.

THE MANAGER

Let us assume a typical situation: a young conductor is engaged as musical director of a relatively unseasoned orchestra whose Board of Directors and Women's Committee are inexperienced with community

---

*Mrs. Thompson has suggested three possible forms of organization: an informal group; an association, separate and distinct from the symphony society with its own constitution and by-laws; and a federation of existing local women's organizations of various kinds. The chapter of her book on Community Symphony Orchestras devoted to Women's Committees is a gold mine of ideas for such auxiliaries.

orchestra business. If the conductor is the one who took the initiative in organizing the orchestra and getting together the Board of Directors and Women's Committee, the conditions will be much the same. Namely, the conductor will find that much of his time and energies will have to be devoted to managing the operation, serving as stagehand, callboy, and general factotum. It is to his advantage, as soon as possible, to secure some kind of volunteer assistance with general management routine and logistics if he is to have much time left at all to devote to musical considerations.

Many orchestras have been able to find very capable individuals who, when called upon from time to time, can greatly assist with management aspects. These nonprofessional managers are valuable, for instance, in giving overall direction to the main drive for contributions, assisting in the detail work of arranging for rehearsal rooms and performing halls, helping with the season-ticket campaign, seeing to it that the box office is staffed for single-ticket sales, making sure that collection plates are available if a free-will offering concert is played, and attending to a host of other details that need attention as the occasion arises.

Ralph Black has succinctly summarized one of the most important roles of the symphony organization—the person who serves as box-office/receptionist. Very often it is here rather than onstage that the orchestra's success or failure is determined. Patrons will tell the box office things they might be afraid to mention to either the conductor or manager. It is the manager's responsibility to provide the staffing for the box office. Be sure that the person assigned is courteous, smiling, pleasant, and mindful of the fact that any single patron is the most important asset in the orchestra business.

Often managers, box-office personnel, and others necessary for the functioning of the orchestra can be found among the non-playing wives or husbands of orchestra members. It gives them a sense of belonging rather than being mere "music widows or widowers." In one orchestra, the part-time manager was the father of one of the younger orchestra members. An orchestra member can also function in this capacity since, most of the time, the manager's duties do not interfere with the rehearsal schedules of most community orchestras.

The manager has loyalty to both board and conductor; these loyalties are sometimes in conflict. The manager should be present at board meetings, but may be in a better position to resolve conflicts between conductor and board if he or she is not a voting member of the board. This will vary from community to community.

It is terribly important that the conductor and manager have a smoothly honed working relationship. While it is obvious that both have their own duties which are mutually exclusive, there are many areas where both must work together in a very smooth way. It is highly important that the working partnership which should exist between the conductor and the manager be one of equality, for as the orchestra grows, it needs even more cooperation between the music and business parts of the association.

Not only must a conductor and manager work together, they must support each other on issues basic to the health of the orchestra. In the event that there is a disagreement, once all the arguments have been pursued and a policy determined by the association, then a united front must be presented. Without it the aims and future of the association will be jeopardized. Should a disagreement be beyond mutual resolution, the board should be the final arbitrator.

As soon as practical, the manager should receive at least a token payment for his or her services. Such generous individuals are often taken for granted; if that happens, the position may come to be taken for granted as well. The services of the manager are highly important and must be given due recognition.

The board should see to it that the conductor, manager, and at least one women's committee member are sent to an American Symphony Orchestra League national conference. Their expenses should be a line item in the orchestra's annual budget. If this is too great a dollar item, at least the nearest of the regional workshops, which are usually closer and of shorter duration, should be considered a "must." Delegates to these conferences and workshops eat, sleep, and breathe symphony orchestra business: the novice manager in particular will benefit greatly by mingling with experts of the symphonic world.

The League also sponsors a training course for orchestra managers for several days each year. These sessions are designed, in part, to help train professional orchestra managers, but smaller orchestras can profit greatly by having their manager attend even one such session. Many graduates of these courses now hold top symphony managerships throughout the country; it is no mere coincidence that nearly all trained orchestra managers have positions, whereas many a trained conductor is looking for work!

In communities where paid stagehands are not available, setting up the orchestra for concerts and rehearsals can be a problem of logistics. This is more acute where the orchestra performs some distance from the rehearsal hall, since there are large instruments which have to be moved and often stands and chairs must be obtained and moved to the performance hall. Many conductors have served their apprentice years moving stands and chairs, but it is not in the best interests of the orchestra that the conductor, who was hired to do a musical job, is also assigned the position of chief furniture mover. "Let it be hoped, however, that the wearer of the manager's hat is *not* the conductor! He has enough to do without that—and he will do it much better if someone relieves him of the management load."[7]

In some cases, for example if the orchestra is performing in a school auditorium, the school will furnish students to serve as stagehands at minimal cost. However, if this is not the case, it is better to seek volunteers from the orchestra family rather than to have either conductor or players do the job.

In conclusion, the conductor, whether forming a new orchestra or working with an existing organization, has three chief aids to his primary job of making music: a Board of Directors which is sympathetic and energetic; a Women's Committee which will be tireless in its work of promoting the orchestra; and some form of managerial assistance which can relieve the conductor of many small details which can become serious problems if neglected.

SUMMARY

We have examined only briefly some of the organizational aspects and responsibilities of the community symphony orchestra and the conductor's relationship to this organizational structure. Strict adherence to the suggestions outlined in this chapter cannot guarantee that an orchestra or conductor will be immediately successful.

There is, however, ample evidence that many of these suggestions will prove to be helpful in aiding the conductor and his orchestra in their common purpose of creating a good musical and artistic atmosphere within the community.

As we shall show in the next chapter, a strong organizational structure can be of great assistance in establishing strong support for the orchestra throughout the entire community.

chapter 2

Community Relations

For most communities, serious music is a needed yet often an unwanted and misunderstood commodity. The conductor in every community must be his orchestra's prime public relations agent. Whether he likes it or not, the conductor's every action must redound to the orchestra's benefit. He is the orchestra's *single image* in the community, and much of the orchestra's success will depend on how that image is projected throughout the entire gamut of the community's life.

The ordering and division of the various segments of a community discussed here is rather arbitrary, being based upon the author's personal experience. The relative importance of the various groups within a community will vary according to location, and the conductor must be able to sense these relative strengths as he moves about and works within the community.

The techniques used by the conductor to sense the attitudes of his community will vary. The most important guideline of all is: *listen!* If the conductor does not listen to and heed what the different segments of his community are saying about the orchestra, about music and other artistic matters, his effectiveness as a purveyor of good music will be severely blunted. A conductor may have many ideas and ideals about what "his" orchestra should be doing within the community; conversely, there is never a community with soul so dead that it does not have ideas, and perhaps ideals, as to what it wants from "its" orchestra. It behooves the conductor not only to keep his ears open, but to encourage and stimulate expression of opinion, for when people talk about something (and feel that someone is listening sympathetically), they begin to feel involved, then interested, and, ultimately, more amenable to suggestions which they would have rejected out-of-hand had they not first had the opportunity to unburden their minds.

If listening is important, so is *patience*. A community that has had no orchestra before, or whose orchestra was not much of a leader in community artistic endeavors, may take a while to grasp the possibilities. While the old saw that "Rome was not built in a day" may no longer be applicable, now that entire communities seem to spring up overnight to the tune of saws and hammers of eager developers, the soul and spirit of a community takes longer to grow.

The young conductor, probably fresh from his training in the big city or big university, must never forget that life in smaller communities tends to be basically conservative in nature. People are living there because they do not want to live in a big city. Whatever culture is going to be developed has to be developed at least partly on their own terms. Having listened, and having certain aims and goals of his own in mind, the conductor must work slowly and steadily if he would build a more enduring success. Patience is the name of the game!

This leads to our third guideline: *persistence*. One must expect a certain amount of resistance to new ideas, especially in smaller communities. Even the idea of having an orchestra at all may not gain wide acceptance at first. There will be doors shut in the conductor's face, but he must not go off in a huff. One must always treat an enemy as if he would one day become a friend. (And following Sophocles' admonition, treat a friend with due precautions against the day when he might become an enemy!) Over and above his own ego, the conductor is in a very real sense a cultural missionary working for a great cause; and the history of good causes has been typified by dedicated persistence, if they are to triumph in the end. Those conductors and boards of directors who have combined patience with persistence and quiet persuasion have succeeded best in achieving effective programs.

THE EDUCATIONAL ESTABLISHMENT

For our purposes, the Educational Establishment may be divided into three groups: educational administration, classroom teachers, and private music teachers. The order in which a conductor approaches each of these will vary from community to community, but experience has shown that classroom teachers are rather likely to follow the lead of the administration. Many of them, to be sure, will be willing volunteers. Military strategy tells us that if we capture the general staff, the foot soldiers will come along more willingly.

The opening approach to the educational administration must be to demonstrate the educational advantages of having an orchestra functioning within the community. If a member of the school administration can be persuaded to serve on the orchestra's board of directors, an effective access channel to public school music personnel in general will have opened up. School administrators for years have been highly receptive to "cultural enrichment," under whatever guise. Even remote small communities on the West Coast have, for many years, used the Standard School Broadcasts as a basis for music appreciation, with the use of classroom time for these broadcasts being encouraged. More recently, the New York Philharmonic Young People's concerts on television have been supported and encouraged by school officials.

The community orchestra should consider presenting school concerts, so that what the youngsters have been hearing out of a loudspeaker at last becomes a real "live" performance. This might be too much to ask if the orchestra is small, or not yet up to its best potential, or if the players would be inconvenienced by having to appear during school hours, or for various other reasons. If one access road is closed, try another! For example, one orchestra, whose concerts were played in a larger hall than its regular audience needed, simply provided a number of seats at these regular concerts to the school district at no charge. The schools furnished transportation and chaperones for the students, and the orchestra's conductor, in conjunction with school music and orchestra personnel, visited each school and discussed the program with the students who were to attend each concert. That this program was successful may be attested to by the fact that many of these school children returned to subsequent concerts bringing parents with them.

Many orchestras price their tickets much lower for students. Some orchestras have admitted students free of charge upon presentation of student identification. Of course, this must be on a "seats available" basis, but for many smaller orchestras there are more seats than ticket purchasers to fill them. This practice can potentially build a future audience for the orchestra. But it is yet too early to measure accurately its effect on audience size. Some other advantages can accrue to the orchestra through cooperation with school administrators: use of larger, school-owned instruments; rehearsal and performance space for minimal or no charge; and, perhaps, an increased awareness on the part of the schools for the need of a strong music program.*

The conductor must carefully avoid giving the impression of either competing with or bypassing public school music teachers. These teachers

---

*Many school districts delay the beginning string program until the junior high school; by the time that those students are proficient enough on their instruments to be of benefit to the community orchestra, they are playing in another orchestra, if at all. Beginning the string instruction in the lower grades can be a goal toward which both orchestra and school administration should strive.

have spent much time preparing for their careers (perhaps as much or more time than many of the younger conductors); they may rightfully resent the newcomer in the community. Community musical development can be wrecked, or severely battered, on the shoals of factionalism. The conductor, as one of the musical leaders in the community, must avoid this sort of conflict.

The training of most conductors has bypassed considerations of music education as a discipline. Ensemble directors and classroom techers have an entirely different set of problems from community orchestra conductors, and it behooves the latter to listen carefully, making every attempt to understand the specific problems of the public school music teacher. He cannot understand them if he is concerned solely with his own orchestra. Enlisting the aid of public school music teachers, a vital asset in any community musical endeavor, will be far easier if the conductor understands the philosophy and purposes of public school music education; understanding comes from careful listening.

Most conductors of major professional symphony orchestras have, as a matter of image, stood somewhat aloof from the give and take of community life and involvement.* Conductors in smaller communities can ill afford this image, and their attempts to ape the personal isolation of the Szells, Reiners, and Toscaninis will not work in a community orchestra situation; especially in working with public school music teachers.

In most smaller communities, the personnel of the community orchestra will include a number of the more advanced student musicians as well as their teachers. For this reason, the support of the school music teacher is vital. The conductor, enlisting the aid of teachers in both recruiting students and playing themselves, must approach them in such a way that the benefit to the teacher and his school program is clear.

The conductor's contacts with the educational community should be on a person-to-person basis. He should consult individually with each of the music teachers in the school system (minding the proverb that "three is a crowd"), at a time convenient to the teacher, to discuss in a spirit of friendly cooperation the general musical climate of the community. Upon such occasions, the conductor must have the common good sense and self-discipline not to be bruiting about things that are said to him in confidence. A good excuse for making such appointments is to express the desire to visit an ensemble in rehearsal, for such a display of interest in the teacher's groups fosters the climate of cooperation. He should also visit the primary music classes, if possible, offering to assist those teachers in any way he can. The classroom teachers, as well as the

*The most notable exceptions are Maurice Abravanel, of the Utah Symphony, and Milton Katims and Rainer Miedel, respectively past and present music directors of the Seattle Symphony.

ensemble leaders, are important resource people for planning school concerts and other educational activities which the community orchestra *should* undertake.

It may be that a youth orchestra, combining advanced instrumentalists from several schools, will help strengthen the school music program, and assist the community orchestra as well. In many communities, the conductor of the adult orchestra serves as conductor of the youth orchestra. If that is not expedient, recruiting the youth orchestra conductor from the school music personnel is advisable. In smaller communities, the establishment of a youth orchestra is best sponsored by the adult orchestra board, rather than by a separate organization.

A very positive approach to the private music teachers and church music staffs is also important; this is often neglected by many conductors. The conductor should get to know each of them as individuals. Although he cannot visit every private music lesson or church service, personal acquaintance with each individual involved is important. The conductor should be interested in the total musical climate of his community (and non-musical climate as well) and not his orchestra alone. While the orchestra is his primary concern, he must remember that to serve the community he must know the *whole* community; the more of it he knows, the better he is able to perform his primary duties. If the conductor seeks out private music teachers, and others involved in music, with the attitude of service for the whole community and of contributing to the strengthening of the musical and artistic climate, he will truly be *serving*, while at the same time making new friends for the orchestra.

We must remember that one good thing leads to another. A strong community orchestra will inevitably encourage more and better activity on the teaching front, whether in the schools or in the private studio. The school orchestra will have a model to look up to. The pianists, violinists, and so on, appearing as soloists with the community orchestra will inspire some boys and girls to practice more diligently in the hope of one day themselves appearing in the spotlight.

RELATIONS WITH THE BUSINESS COMMUNITY

Before the conductor moves to a new community, he must have a good understanding of its business and industrial base. Much information can be supplied by the local chamber of commerce. The conductor should quickly become familiar with the banking and financial institutions, the manufacturing industry, retail stores and smaller service businesses. *In short, the more he knows his community, the better he can serve it.*

Fund-raising must not be the primary task of the conductor, even though he often finds himself doing just that. One simply does not walk up to a stranger with outstretched hand, expecting a donation. The common sense of human relations dictates that we first of all extend the hand of genuine, friendly interest in our neighbors—and these include the businesses and industries of the smaller city. There is plenty of time, after one has become friends, to request favors. Many industrial firms, for example, provide scheduled tours of their operations for those interested: the conductor would be well advised to take advantage of such opportunities. In doing so, he acquires a better understanding of the activities around him and, believe me, his interest will not pass unnoticed!

That the money needs of an orchestra are important, no one can deny. There is perhaps more literature devoted to arts funding than to almost any other aspect of cultural organization. The conductor should recognize how, and from whom, his orchestra raises money even though it is not his first responsibility.

Involvement by business with artistic endeavors is growing, not only in financial support but also through the lending of executives for special projects. In their definitive study on arts funding, William Baumol and William Bowen have stated: "Corporations have been formalizing their giving in other ways as well: through the establishment of contributions committees, the assignment of full-time employees to deal with contribution matters, and through the preparation of explicit contribution budgets."[1] An added benefit to corporations and other businesses is that they can enjoy some of the same tax advantages from contributing to the arts as can individuals.*

If the orchestra is already established, many of the mechanics for funding will already be in operation. With a new orchestra, on the other hand, the conductor needs to be aware of some of the procedures which have been effective for other orchestras. In this respect, too, the American Symphony Orchestra League can be of assistance.

In most communities, the chamber of commerce can be one of the best allies a conductor and his orchestra can have. Many chambers maintain a community calendar for all events within the community; the orchestra must be a part of it. Business firms may have pooled resources for such items as public service advertisements and contributions through chambers of commerce.

> A survey of 147 chambers conducted by *Arts Management*, a newsletter for the executives of cultural institutions, found that nearly one out of every five chambers made direct financial contributions to local arts groups, and fully four out of five provided rent-free space, handled mailings, donated printing or other services to them.[2]

*Revisions of the Internal Revenue Code in 1935 introduced a provision whereby corporations and businesses could deduct up to a maximum of 5 percent of their pretax profits for charitable contributions.

An invitation to address a luncheon meeting of the chamber must be high on the conductor's list of priorities. Once the invitation is secured, great care must go into formulating his remarks. The conductor must be prepared to discuss why the orchestra and its growth will be good for the community as a whole, and he must be able to show, either publicly or privately, that the orchestra's financial arrangements are solidly based on good accounting practices. Baumol and Bowen have pointed out that "there is the view that one of the main handicaps of many performing organizations is their relatively unbusinesslike organization and administration. . . ."[3] Thus, an additional argument for a very strong and effective organization and administration for the orchestra. One conductor recently observed privately that his sole address for a number of years to various service organizations was entitled "Good Music Is Good Business," wherein he pointed out to his listeners that a growing cultural climate in the community was beneficial to all areas of community life.

The conductor should slant his remarks toward the special interests of the group he is addressing: some are youth-assistance oriented, others stress help to medical service units, and so on. For example, when speaking to youth-oriented groups, the conductor might stress school concerts and young musician participation in the orchestra as two topics which can engender interest in, and support for, the orchestra.

Business and industry are rapidly decentralizing their operations. Due to more rapid transportation and communications, many areas of the country which were once solely dependent on agriculture are now discovering new industries in their midst. This influx of certain types of industry has helped the growth of all areas of community life, including cultural pursuits.

Before an industry or business moves into a new community, that community must have certain attributes which will be attractive to new residents. Good schools, recreational facilities, and a rewarding cultural environment are some of the elements sought.

Even if an executive never goes to the theatre himself, he may well be glad to be reassured that he is not establishing his new plant in a cultural desert and he can use the existence of the theatre (or symphony orchestra) as an inducement to attract new personnel to work for him.[4]

If the orchestra is playing a vital role in a community, new business and industry will find that community more attractive.

Professional people—doctors, dentists, lawyers, accountants—have had a long history of involvement with artistic endeavors, as witness doctors' orchestras in Chicago, New York, Philadelphia, and Los Angeles. A cursory glance at audience surveys shows that the average arts consumer has attained a higher degree of education than the national average, which would include the legal, dental, and medical professions.

> Our culture consumer, it will be no surprise to learn, is also far better educated than the man in the street. He may not have completed college, but the odds are roughly four out of five that he has had at least some exposure to higher education or that the head of his household has. The *Bravo* concert hall study and the Guthrie theater audience study both found that between 80 and 83 per cent of those in their audience had attended college or were members of families headed by a person who had been to college.[5]
>
> We conclude that the audience is composed of *exceedingly* well-educated persons. Less than 3 per cent of the males and females did not graduate from high school, as compared to more than 50 per cent of the U.S. urban population 25 years and over who did not do so. At the other end of the spectrum, over 55 per cent of the males attending performances did some work beyond college—an educational level attained by only 5 percent of the urban population.[6]

Keeping in mind that present-day audiences tend to be made up of more highly educated persons, nevertheless we must continue to encourage other, less well-educated persons to attend concerts and other cultural events as well.

Contributors' lists of most orchestras demonstrate the willingness of professional people to become financially involved with cultural growth in addition to attending concerts and plays. Higher degrees of educational attainment usually indicate higher income brackets; it is especially important for the orchestra to have a tax-exempt status so that major contributors have some tax advantage.

The religious community must not be overlooked. From a public-relations and concert-promotion standpoint (not a financial one), the churches can be helpful to the orchestra. Church bulletins and newsletters can serve to promote concert attendance; choirs can unite for oratorio performances with the orchestra; rehearsal space, often at minimal fees, may be obtained in church buildings. These are but three ways which the community's churches can help. Further, it is as important for the conductor to meet the ministers as it is to cultivate the acquaintance of business and professional leaders.

A word of caution: to every extent possible, the conductor's personal expenditures should be made within the community that supports him.

After all, he expects the community's patronage; why should they not expect his? Not to buy locally skates along the thin edge of disloyalty.

In summary, the conductor will be able to create support for his orchestra from the business, professional, and religious leaders in his community by listening to their desires and interests and addressing them with *their* problems in mind, by knowing as much about the business and industrial base of his community as he can, and by becoming as involved as possible in the community himself, including buying locally.

RELATIONS WITH THE MEDIA

A close rapport with the press, radio, and television is vital for the conductor and his orchestra. Whether one is recruiting players, building an audience, or raising money, the respective media can be strong allies. It is vital for the conductor to be freely available to them, not only in terms of his musical leadership, but by being known to people working in public information areas which will help bring the conductor closer to the community.

Relations with the press require diligent cultivation; many people in a community rely on what they read rather than what they hear on radio or television. The conductor should know not only the arts and music editor, but the editor of the women's page and the general editorial staff as well.

It is the conductor who must cultivate these relationships. Rarely will he be sought out save for an occasional interview. The conductor must lead, and his leadership will not be effective if his relations with the press are limited to occasional interviews with the music critic.

Several conductors serve as columnists with smaller daily papers, on a weekly or some other basis. Their columns deal with almost any subject concerning the orchestra, music in general, or common community efforts. The column must always redound to the orchestra's benefit, and the use of columnist's prerogative to expound on issues which might incur displeasure of any of the orchestra's supporters cannot be allowed.

From time to time, the conductor may be asked to serve as a music critic. Although he can perform a service here, since most smaller newspapers do not have musically trained individuals available, he should resist such invitations. Any ill-feelings arising from such criticism may cause damage to the orchestra and its image in the community.

Most newspapers will cover worthwhile local enterprises to the extent of available space. Good lines of communication between the conductor and the press can increase this coverage. Good relations with the press include buying advertising for the orchestra. In communities where the conductor is also a private music teacher, taking an advertisement announcing registration of new students will be considered a gesture of goodwill by the newspaper.

Press releases are an invaluable aid in making the community aware of the orchestra and its activities. The conductor should *not* be the one responsible for their preparation, but he can assist the person(s) assigned to prepare them. Press releases should not be overly long, but should contain the necessary information in readable form. Recruiting a board member from among the public information media can be helpful.

Publicity campaigns must be through the most widely read, viewed, or heard outlets. Often the minor newspapers and shopping-news weeklies are overlooked: they serve an audience and advertising should be purchased from them as well as using them as vehicles for general news releases.

There are several ways the conductor can exploit radio and television. Some conductors serve as "disc jockeys" on radio stations, playing recordings of works to be performed at forthcoming concerts. Here the conductor can discuss the music, present pertinent background information about the composer, and interview orchestra musicians and soloists. The conductor becomes a "voice" as well as the back of a full-dress suit. Since radio personalities tend to build a personal following, the conductor may become identifiable to the general public, often not concert goers, whose curiosity is piqued so that they want to *see* the voice they have been hearing. Even if the conductor does not care to become regularly involved as disc jockey, an occasional guest appearance might be arranged, perhaps at some stipulated time—for instance, immediately prior to concerts—to which his "friends of the air" could look forward with anticipation.

The conductor need not always wait to be asked to do such programs: many stations are looking for local source material and talent. Two cautions to the conductor in this regard: he should not be required to read high-pressure advertising material if his program is sponsored; and if the community boasts more than one radio station, the outlet with a more adult audience would be the better to approach.

Obviously, this kind of program format is not suitable for television. But television should not be overlooked. For instance, a program using musicians from the orchestra can help "personalize" members of the orchestra to an audience. Such programming must have a content with broad appeal so that viewers will not become bored and switch channels. Approval from the musicians' union local must be obtained in advance for any kind of live or taped program involving performing musicians.

One publicity area often overlooked is the "foreign" radio station or newspaper. Many orchestras are located within hearing distance of metropolitan radio stations which broadcast arts-events calendars daily or weekly. Most of those stations are looking for material for public service announcements. It is an added psychological benefit for regular patrons of the orchestra when "their" orchestra is mentioned in a newspaper or on radio from afar. Public service announcements are usually broadcast without cost.

An additional outlet for publicity and promotion that should not be neglected is church bulletins and newsletters. Pastors of churches within a community are usually happy to call concerts to the attention of their parishioners, especially if the program has a religious content such as an oratorio performance.

Posters of various kinds can be a useful means of promotion, provided they are attractive and state the necessary information with a minimum of words. If there is no daily newspaper, posters become an essential means of bridging the information gap which occurs between issues of a weekly paper. Poster location is very important: a few posters spotted around where there is heavy foot-traffic will be more effective than a large number in less strategic locations. Posters in business establishments must be there with the permission of the business person.

In conclusion, the many public information media can be the best advertisement for the orchestra. Publicity materials should not be the primary responsibility of the conductor, but he must be willing and ready to be of assistance to the publicity chairperson or committee of the orchestra. Non-local media should also be used. Church bulletins, posters, school announcements and minor newspapers can also help increase the audience for the orchestra.

RELATIONS WITH OTHER ARTS ORGANIZATIONS

A conductor moving into a new community or starting a new orchestra must establish a good working relationship with other cultural organizations. Community theaters, other concert series, art leagues, and many more organizations serve the community and perhaps the orchestra; multilateral collaboration will expedite the good cultural life for all citizens.

A community-events calendar helps keep performance schedules straight and avoids unnecessary conflicts. Non-cultural events should also be kept in mind; for instance, if the high school basketball team draws large turnouts, fewer people will come to concerts that are held on game nights.

If there is not already some type of community arts council, one should be speedily formed, with the conductor taking an interested and vital part. Community arts councils have helped in areas of fund-raising, audience growth, and general community awareness of common artistic goals and endeavors.

Between 1946 and 1950 arts councils were formed in eight American cities. By 1955 their number had multiplied to 25. Today (1964) arts councils already exist in 125 communities from Jacksonville, Florida, to Tacoma, Washington, and new ones are forming all the time. An additional 35 councils have sprung up across the border in Canada.[7]

Baumol and Bowen have stated a case for arts councils:

Thus, united fund raising efforts can be effective if the leaders are careful to avoid the reported tendency of community arts councils to sponsor the routine and shy away from experimental efforts. If these groups can also maintain the autonomy and zeal of their constituent organizations, they may prove an important financial instrument for the performing arts. Fund raising is a difficult task, and arts councils can perhaps provide a vehicle for more skillful planning, execution and coordinating of fund raising efforts for many small institutions, which, left to themselves, might find it too difficult a task.[8]

But arts councils are not necessarily the solution in every community. A particular group may have built up its own following to the extent that combining forces with other organizations will not be to its advantage. In that case, that is where a formal alliance may not be deemed desirable, there is still the possibility of mutual cooperation on specific individual projects.

The American Symphony Orchestra League has published information which outlines the procedures proven successful in forming arts councils, together with a survey detailing the organizational structure, bylaws, and constituent groups of sixteen such councils.[9]

Special consideration must be given to civic music associations or Community Concerts series, whose purpose is to bring traveling attractions to pre-sold audiences. Their dates are determined as much by the availability of the artists as by community convenience. Once more, the community-events calendar can help avoid conflicts. The orchestra may, for instance, have to postpone a concert or relinquish a specific date, but planning ahead can reduce this problem to a minimum. If an orchestra date has to be changed, change the date with good grace!* Community Concerts is not a competing but a corollary group, often less flexible than local organizations.

Whether the formation of an arts council is desirable will vary from community to community, but the conductor and his board must keep themselves open to all possible avenues of cooperation.

RELATIONS WITH THE AMERICAN FEDERATION OF MUSICIANS

All players in professional orchestras, including conductors, belong to the American Federation of Musicians. A visit to the local secretary of the A. F. of M. will provide the necessary information about local regulations concerning union musicians playing in nonprofessional orchestras. The secretary can also assist in player recruitment. It will be helpful if the conductor makes early application for his own membership in the local.

Recording rehearsals and performances should in no case be made operational without prior clearance from the union. The by-laws of the Federation speak to this problem in general terms; each jurisdiction usually has its own specific rulings on recording rehearsals and performances. The conductor must be sure he understands all local regulations. Particular attention should be given to the copyright law of 1976 as it relates to recording. There are several new provisions with which all orchestras should be familiar.

One other aspect of the activities of the A. F. of M. is the Congress of Strings, an eight-week training program for talented young string players. The participants in the Congress are chosen by auditions administered by each local of the Federation. Winners are provided transportation, board and room. The Congress is held at two sites (College/Conservatory of Music of the University of Cincinnati in Ohio, and the University of Washington in Seattle). The assignment to one or the other site depends on travel distance and balance of instrumentation.

The Congress sessions are devoted to a daily string orchestra rehearsal, private lessons with distinguished faculty, and intensive chamber music experience. There are four public concerts during the session; conductors for these concerts, selected by the Federation, have included such notable maestri as Alfred Wallenstein, Eugene Ormandy, Milton Katims, Samuel Krachmalnick, and Harold Farberman.

*Many orchestra members will doubtless hold memberships in Community Concerts. This may prove a problem if these touring attractions happen to appear on an orchestral rehearsal evening. The rehearsal should be rescheduled if such a conflict arises.

Community orchestras should be alert to the obvious advantages of this program for their own needs and should actively seek the cooperation of their own locals in promoting auditions and scholarships.

SUMMARY

The conductor should meet his community as soon as possible: educational leaders, business and professional people, public information media, and other persons interested in cultural pursuits. It is most important that no part of the community be overlooked; if one or more of these populations is slighted in any way, it is doubly difficult to enlist or reenlist their aid.

chapter 3

Orchestra Operations

The *raison d'être* of any orchestra is the making of music. This activity necessarily is supported by a number of routine operations upon which the efficiency of the orchestra will largely depend. There must be some basic library of scores and parts, properly cared for. Arrangements have to be made with rental agencies and licensing agencies for desired materials not in the basic library. Equipment for rehearsals and concerts must be procured. There is the question of what players shall wear for concerts. Arrangements must be made for the care, storage, and repair (when needed) of larger instruments owned by the orchestra, not excluding a good concert grand piano. Someone must contract with soloists or other imported players and see that they are made comfortable upon arrival. The logistics involved when the orchestra moves momentarily to some other locale than the usual one must be tended to. And so on and on. While specific situations will vary from orchestra to orchestra, certain basic considerations must be kept in mind.

THE LIBRARY

As soon as the conductor has a mailing address in the community, it would be advisable for him to write to publishers requesting catalogues and inclusion on mailing lists. This will enable him to assist the librarian in locating necessary materials. (See Appendix C for addresses.)

The library is strategic to the musical life of the orchestra. Proper care and storage of parts is a primary consideration. Nothing can be more frustrating for the conductor or the players than to put a set of parts on the stands and find that wind or brass parts are missing. String parts are less of a problem, since extra copies should have been purchased in the first place or, if the parts are in the public domain, extra copies can be run off on a good copying machine. (Whereas if a first horn part is missing, there is nothing to copy!)

Various types of storage boxes or envelopes are available from most music supply houses.[1] Efficiency will be promoted by some uniformity in the storage system. It is well to plan ahead (keeping future growth in mind) and do it properly from the start. For instance, storage boxes measuring 11½ by 15 inches (the proper size to hold the older and larger Breitkopf and Härtel parts) will not fit upright in a legal-size filing cabinet. Those boxes must be put into the file drawers at an angle; since they will become damaged as the drawers are opened and closed, they are best stored flat or on edge on shelves. The 9½- by 12-inch box will fit in a legal-size cabinet. Single-fold manila folders used in file drawers are not too successful since individual parts tend to squeeze upward and become torn as the drawer is opened and closed. A closed-flap, heavy-duty, adequately labeled envelope is more satisfactory in filing cabinets.

The library should be located either with the conductor or with a board member, unless the orchestra can afford to rent space for it. It is not advisable for an orchestra member to store the library unless he or she is also the librarian.

Library inventory need not be elaborate. The University of Washington orchestra library uses a duplicate card system of inventory control (one copy in the library, one for the conductor) with no listing of individual parts on the storage boxes. Cards are easy to manipulate, and should the conductor need to know if parts for a work are available, he can look at his copy of the file. (In the case of a college or university orchestra, it is better that the orchestral parts library be completely separate from the filling system of the main school or departmental library, thus the elaborate cataloguing procedure is not involved.)

The Port Angeles Symphony Orchestra has an even simpler operation. This community orchestra owns approximately one hundred sets of parts, which are kept in the conductor's home. A card file of the library lists only title, composer, publisher, and number and distribution of parts. Involved cataloguing is not necessary since the library is noncirculating.

The role of the librarian is highly important, whatever the size of the orchestra. Bowings and fingerings decided upon by the conductor or his principal players should be marked into the parts by the librarian, who must be a sufficiently capable musician to do this properly. Naturally, the librarian must pass out parts before rehearsals and collect them afterward. When parts are needed by players to take home for practice, these must be efficiently checked out and kept track of. In general, it devolves upon the librarian to keep the library in good order to minimize loss or damage to the materials.

Parts should be marked only with a soft lead pencil—never with colored pencil or ballpoint pen! All markings should be considered temporary: one never knows when they might need to be changed. Further, the parts will need to be cleaned before they are returned to rental libraries.* It is therefore to the librarian's advantage (and the convenience of the players) if each stand is supplied with a soft lead pencil.

Regarding this question of marking parts, a word of general advice is in order: it must be remembered that community orchestra string players are not usually of professional caliber. Bowings and fingerings that would prove effective, say, for the Cleveland Orchestra are not necessarily suitable for the string players of a community orchestra. Effects produced by a string section are cumulative, bearing in mind the lowest common denominator—the weakest player. Anything else will lead to a scrambling of bows and lack of clarity in execution. The conductor must be most careful about being the one to determine bowings and fingerings, particularly if he is an accomplished string player. It is better to let the principal string player do the bowings and fingerings in most community orchestras, since he or she is, or should be, more cognizant of the strengths and weaknesses of the string section.

The conductor must stress to all the players the urgency of taking care of parts used for practice at home. If players sharing a set of parts desire to divide the music for individual practice, it is their responsibility to see to it that all of the music is back in the folder for the next rehearsal. A clever librarian can devise a suitable checkout system to keep track of the parts.

The conductor should consider carefully when to purchase music for the permanent library and when to rent. Rental charges from most rental libraries are usually nominal; unless a work is to be performed rather frequently, it would be wiser to rent than to purchase. Appendix C provides the names and addresses of the more widely utilized rental libraries and publishers. Most libraries rent music on a monthly basis and often provide a grace period of a few additional days to allow for delays in the mails.

---

*The orchestra might consider purchasing an electric eraser, such as those used in libraries, for the librarian for the purpose of cleaning rented parts before they are returned. The harder erasers used by libraries for erasing catalogue cards are not advisable for use on music. The soft, silicon erasers will not tear the paper as the harder ones do. It is also very important that if the librarian does not have a real working knowledge of the several languages which are used to identify orchestral instruments, a small musical dictionary should be provided. Nothing disturbs rehearsals more than having the tromba (trumpet) parts on the trombone stands, the corno (horn) parts on the trumpet stands, and no one knowing where the posaune (trombones) should go.

Some orchestral works (for example, the early symphonies of Dvořák) are not available from most commercial libraries. Many of these can be had on loan from the Fleischer Collection of the Philadelphia Free Library. The catalogue of this collection may be found in larger city or university library reference departments.

The parts for contemporary works are not available for purchase and must be rented from the composer's publisher. Publishing house information on contemporary works is available from either the Broadcast Music, Incorporated (BMI) or the American Society of Composers, Authors and Publishers (ASCAP) symphonic catalogues.

The conductor planning to perform a number of contemporary works will save money if the orchestra applies for blanket performance licenses from either BMI or ASCAP or both. The fees for these licenses are scaled according to the orchestra budget, auditorium size, ticket prices, and number of concerts per year. Licensing agreements cover only the performance fees (royalties), not the rental of the materials, and do not apply to staged works or orchestral works over forty minutes in duration.*

THE REHEARSAL ROOM

A word about the rehearsal room is necessary. It is very important that the sight lines are clear so that the conductor can see all of the players and the players are able to see the conductor. Bad lighting and bad ventilation can bring bad sounds from an orchestra. If lighting and ventilation problems cannot be corrected easily, look for another rehearsal room. The room should also have sufficient storage to take care of any large instruments owned by the orchestra and a lockable area for music and other equipment used solely by the orchestra, such as stands and chairs.

The chairs used in rehearsals should have level seats and be of the stacking rather than the folding kind. Chair seats which tilt toward the back at an angle do not provide the proper breath support for wind and brass players, are awkward for cellists, and lead to physical fatigue for the players which will adversely affect the making of music.

It is important to have handy a good blackboard with ample chalk and erasers. Very often the conductor can make good teaching points in very little time by using a blackboard. A sage observed that ''a picture is worth a thousand words'' and personal experience of the author has demonstrated time and again the wisdom of that observation.

The practice of tape recording rehearsals should be used very sparingly. While a tape playback of a section of a rehearsal can be of help on rare occasions, unless the equipment available is of better than average

---

*The forty-minute time limit applies to works licensed by BMI only; ASCAP has no time limit on purely orchestral works.

quality, the experience can be more frustrating than helpful. Also, too much use of a tape recorder during rehearsals can use up much of the already inadequate rehearsal time.

Many rehearsal rooms have such peculiar acoustics that the conductor cannot hear the orchestra properly. Unless the room is arranged with fixed risers, this problem can sometimes be solved by rotating the orchestra by ninety degrees in one direction or the other. It is possible that poor acoustics cannot be improved even with some treatment to the room; if that is the case, a new rehearsal area should be sought.

Finally, the rehearsal room must have some sort of temperature control so that when extreme weather conditions prevail, the players can remain comfortable while rehearsing.

PERFORMANCE HALL AND STAGE SETUP

Most community orchestras are forced to rehearse in a location other than the concert hall, which, however, ought to be available for a dress rehearsal before each actual performance. The acoustics of the rehearsal hall may be good or bad. If good, the conductor is indeed fortunate; if bad, a vigorous attempt should be made to secure a more suitable location. As for the dress rehearsal (more than one would be preferable), the conductor and orchestra will have to adjust to the acoustics of the *empty* hall and then make further adjustment when an audience is present. The final decision must come from experimentation in the concert hall.

Recording all or part of a dress rehearsal in the hall, or inviting a hi-fi enthusiast or other sound-oriented individual to the rehearsal can help the conductor determine the sound in the auditorium. Orchestra arrangement is the conductor's responsibility: whether the cellos, violas, or second violins are on the outside at the conductor's right is his choice. It may be found, however, that changing one section around may improve the sound.

Maestro Leopold Stokowski experimented over many years with various orchestra seating arrangements. While making these experiments, he always checked the sound with microphone and earphones since the conductor's position is not always the best place to judge. Community orchestra viola sections are generally weaker than cello sections; it is thus better to place them inside the cellos so that the "f" holes of the instruments are more directly pointed toward the audience. If all string sections are weak, particularly second violins and violas, it is usually better to keep the winds and brass on the floor rather than on risers so that some of their penetration will be into the backs of the string players. Community orchestra trumpet players, for example, should be encouraged to keep the bells of their instruments pointed directly at the music stand in front of them. Less experienced flute players have problems projecting the lower notes which they are often required to play; they should either be elevated or have lower flute notes doubled. (Many community orchestras have more flutes available than usually needed, so it is a way of keeping them busy.)

Major changes of stage setup to achieve desired balance cannot be made between pieces on the program. If the woodwinds are on risers for the Beethoven overture, they must remain there for the remainder of the program. Setting of shells, placing and removing of risers except at regular intermissions causes too much visible confusion and the audience loses much of its enthusiasm and interest. In short, during a performance, onstage activity between works *must* be kept to an absolute minimum.*

PLANNING NEW FACILITIES

If a new hall is in the planning stage, the conductor should be involved in such planning at least insofar as the orchestra's use of the facility is concerned. New facilities can provide the conductor additional programming possibilities such as opera, large choral works, and musicals. It is to his advantage to become involved in the early planning for such facilities.

While the conductor cannot be expected to be an expert in acoustics or architecture, he ought to be at least sufficiently well grounded in the principles to offer some good commonsense advice. There are many sources of information for these matters: the physics departments of nearby colleges or universities, the *Journal of the Acoustical Society of America*, and *Architectural Forum*, not to mention site visits to completed auditoriums in the area.[2]

Most new facilities have the nature of multi-purpose buildings; care must be taken to insure that the hall has adequate storage, doorways through which pianos can be moved easily, and other similar features which contribute to easy use of the hall and the comfort of the performers.

There are many school facilities in the planning and construction stage at the present time. It is frightening to consider the amount of money that could be wasted upon improperly designed facilities in those buildings, upon facilities that are not suited for their particular situations, or upon facilities that are designed to suit specific situations that are not appropriate to their particular communities.

*For this reason, it is wise to schedule a piano concerto either immediately before or immediately after intermission so that the audience is forced to witness only one of the piano moves, rather than both of them.

An auditorium should be designed so that the activities can be maintained and operated with a minimum of time and labor consumed in the preparation of an event. In schools this area is being designed for education, not commercial purposes. Architects with experience in designing neighborhood motion picture theaters are not necessarily prepared to solve the problems associated with school auditorium.[3]

In planning for the new hall, the conductor, together with community theater representatives, can help with the layout of backstage facilities. Stage wings which are not large enough for more than a handful of people make concert intermissions a traffic jam. Likewise, unless some consideration is given to the pit area, the conductor's hopes of opera or other musical-dramatic performances will have to be put aside.[4] Consideration should also be given to adequate dressing rooms, lavatories, and drinking fountains backstage. Nothing is more frustrating for singers and instrumentalists than not being able to get a quick drink of water before going onstage.

A common fault of school auditoriums is that the lavatories and public rooms are often quite a distance from the auditorium. In some instances they can even be in other parts of the building which are locked, so that there is no access to them during theatre performances.[5]

ORCHESTRA DRESS

There was a time when orchestra players were expected to wear nothing but solid black. In the 1970s fashions began to change for orchestra members. As early as 1971, a fashion show at the American Symphony Orchestra League National Conference in Seattle, Washington, displayed the "new look" in orchestra dress for women. It was apparent that "solemn black" was no longer the model!

Where tuxedos are a dress tradition in a community, male orchestra members might consider this possibility. Otherwise, dark suits with four-in-hand ties are in best keeping with an orchestra devoted to serious music. Most communities seem to prefer that the conductor wear tails for evening concerts. The conductor might, however, ask his board members about their preferences.

Uniformity in women's and men's dress tends to blend individuals into the whole orchestra. It may be distracting for an audience to find a wide variety in styles and colors. Many orchestras have found, however, that a basic style in a limited variety of subdued colors has the desired effect. Further, a rather simple pattern can be selected and individually sewn rather inexpensively.

Dress length is very important. When skirts are short, they can be distracting to an audience, particularly if the orchestra is on risers, and to the conductor and other players as well.

Orchestra dress need not be drab or unstylish. Perhaps the best solution is for the players to select a committee to work out designs and colors. All age groups within the orchestra should be represented on such a committee.

ORCHESTRA PROGRAMS

The programs passed out by the ushers are important for the orchestra. They must be attractive, provide the necessary information, and be easy to read. It is vital that the spelling of all names be accurate. It will be up to the board to determine whether advertising will be sold in the programs, whether programs will be printed or reproduced by other means, and whether program notes will be included.

Conductors may wish to write the program notes themselves; after all, they should know more about the music than anyone else. On the other hand, it may be prudent to enlist a faculty member of a nearby college or university to provide this service. From whatever source, program notes will increase audience enjoyment of the music and should be provided.

IMPORTED PLAYERS*

Many smaller communities lack English horns, harps, and other less common (though often used) instruments, or they lack sufficient strength in string sections and must therefore augment their own complements with additional players. Usually these players must be imported from neighboring metropolitan areas. This practice can present some problems. The resident players may welcome the additional musicians because they realize that adding key people will strengthen the group as a whole. On the other hand, there can be some resentment, since imported players often must be paid. This problem must be resolved. It will be up to both the conductor and the board of directors to resolve it in such a way that the resident members remain content. The orchestra functions for the resident members—not for the imported musicians, no matter how important or highly skilled they may be. The conductor can help solve the problem in advance by explaining to the players the necessity

*Local vs. imported *soloists* will be discussed in Chapter 4.

for importing extra people. It is also well realize that imported string players will create fewer resentments if they are placed well within a section and not on the first stands.

The pay scale for imported players, most of whom will be musicians' union members, must be determined through the cooperation of both union and players. The conductor should project his needs for imported players at the time when the season's budget is being prepared, otherwise a sudden bill for reimbursement of added musicians might come as an unwelcome surprise to the board.

If he finds that the needs of the music can be served adequately by not utilizing all of the funds appropriated for this purpose, so much the better: a surplus of funds in any budget category is always welcome news to an orchestra board.

ORCHESTRA-OWNED INSTRUMENTS

The orchestra, its conductor and board, should give some consideration to purchasing gradually some of the larger instruments which are not owned by individual players. Celeste, timpani, gong, mallet percussion instruments, English horn, and an extra string bass are some instruments which a community orchestra should consider owning.

The orchestra budget should provide some reserve funds for this purpose. These instruments are expensive and their purchase should be weighed against possible needs. However, there may come a time when "making do" will not be sufficient; to hold both orchestra and audience, these instruments should be available.

If the community does not have an adequate concert grand piano in its auditorium, consideration should be given to a united effort by several organizations (orchestra, Community Concerts, public schools) to purchase a fine piano for all concerts. Here is another example of the need for arts council cooperation.

MISCELLANEOUS CONSIDERATIONS

The length of the orchestral season will vary from community to community. A conductor new to an already established orchestra will tailor his programming to the number of concerts already established in previous seasons, whereas with a newly formed orchestra, the number of concerts will depend on a number of considerations which must be resolved by trial and error.

The number of rehearsals needed for each concert will be determined by the orchestra itself. In the case of a newly formed orchestra, however, the conductor must bear in mind that an ideal rehearsal-to-concert ratio may be found. The author's own experience has been that fewer than six rehearsals tend to leave too many threads dangling, contributing to insecurity, and more than eight or nine rehearsals can lead to boredom and lackluster rehearsals. Usually the concerts end up in good shape, but the wear and tear on the conductor striving to overcome the letdown during the large number of rehearsals is great.

Absenteeism is another problem which the conductor must face squarely. Obviously illnesses, family emergencies, and last-minute transportation breakdowns do occur, and the conductor who is understanding of these legitimate problems will create a climate of goodwill among his players. Conversely, the conductor who condones flagrant and repeated absences from rehearsals or is insensitive to legitimate absences will have a morale problem difficult to solve. Another instance where common sense must prevail.

An effective device to counteract the "summer slump" when the orchestra is on vacation is a series of newsletters to the players that keeps them posted on plans for the ensuing season and includes any other information which may be of interest. This keeps the interest up even though no rehearsals are taking place. Some community orchestras are able to provide summer concerts for their communities, but most of the smaller orchestras cannot keep the necessary personnel intact through the vacation period to present programs up to the caliber of the regular season's offerings.

While the summer will be vacation time for the conductor as well, it can provide him with some additional time to prepare the following season's programs, help the librarian locate needed materials, and assist the orchestra's administration in many ways. This can be a good time to take care of some of the things which get put off during the rush of the orchestra's full schedule in the fall.

SUMMARY

Some of the techniques of orchestra operations which will enhance the total effect of the orchestra include an efficiently operated and ever-expanding orchestra library, a rehearsal room which is convenient, and performances which are enjoyable to see as well as hear. The conductor should be prepared to assist in the planning for new performing facilities. He should also be able to argue effectively for expenditures for imported players and the purchase of instruments as the need arises.

The orchestra's showcase consists of its public performances; these must be backed up by smoothly functioning operations that insure "all systems go" at the precise moment they are needed. Nothing can degrade an orchestra's stature quite like unpreparedness: last-minute corrections of errors that slipped by, or hastily improvised adjustments to repair what was plain lack of foresight.

chapter 4

Conducting as Art and Craft

Although this guide is not designed as a treatise on conducting as an art or craft, yet certain requirements must be met and traits acquired by those desiring to be conductors. As Berlioz wrote so eloquently:

> Among creative artists the composer is almost the only one depending upon a host of intermediaries between him and the public —intermediaries who may be intelligent or stupid, friendly or hostile, diligent or negligent. It is in their power either to carry his work on to brilliant success or to disfigure, debase or even destroy it.
>
> Singers are often considered the most dangerous of these intermediaries; I believe that this is not true. In my opinion, the conductor is the one whom the composer has most to fear.[1]

to which Verdi added the remark, "Once we had to bear the tyranny of the prima donnas; now comes that of the conductors as well!"[2]

For the conductor, then, to avoid the wrath of composers both past and present, he would be well advised to meet with all honesty those requirements and acquire with all sincerity those traits which have historically marked the most loved and respected of conductors.

ON CONDUCTING TECHNIQUE

Most of the books written on conducting limit their discussions to matters of conducting technique, and rightly so. Technique is a vital part of the conductor's training. Without a clear beat which communicates not only metrical messages but the character and style of playing desired at any given point, the conductor wastes rehearsal time talking.

Whether or not conducting can indeed be taught has been debated for years. Eugene Ormandy has been quoted on the subject as follows:

> Conducting cannot be taught. If you go into the history of great conductors you will find that none of them had conducting lessons as such. They all grew up as orchestral musicians and because of their inborn talent for conducting, when the opportunity presented itself, often unexpectedly, they were ready to step on the podium. A possible exception to this theory is Mr. Stokowski, who was a church organist before he became a conductor.[3]

Carl Bamberger perhaps modified Ormandy's position somewhat when he wrote: "The methods, techniques, and approaches expounded by the experts, the conductors themselves, probably have as many variations as there are practitioners of this most intangible of interpretive functions. They do, however, seem to agree on one thing: *the skill of conducting can be learned, but not the art.*"[4] (Emphasis added.) Leopold Stokowski stated the problem perhaps more emphatically than anyone else when he said, "Conductors are born, not made. No amount of academic education can make a real conductor out of someone who is not born with the necessary qualities."[5]

Just as the development of an adequate keyboard technique is necessary for the performance of Beethoven sonatas, so is an adequate conducting technique mandatory for leading on orchestra in concise and cohesive performances. The fledgling conductor (too often the one entrusted with the leadership of community orchestras) must master the rudiments of conducting technique—the historic beat of patterns, the judicious use of the left hand, and the importance of maintaining eye contact with his players.

The late Hermann Scherchen most fervently stated the case for student conductors developing their technique.

> When the student confronts an orchestra, he must be fully equipped in the matter of technique. He must not be capable only of using with utmost accuracy the processes of his craft, but must know how to subordinate the orchestra's multiple personality to his own conception of the work.[6]

The act of conducting can be defined as follows: gestures, the conductor's one and only medium during performance, must indicate perfectly clearly the metrical course of the work; and at the same time, it must convey in unequivocal fashion the varying expression and general shaping of the work. But the first requirement is that the metrical picture should remain the same and equally clear, whether the motions be large or small, slow or fast, vehement or tender.[7]

When a student confronts an orchestra for the first time, he must have thoroughly mastered the practice of his craft. He must be not merely theoretically able to conduct an orchestra, but *actually capable of dealing with the realities of the orchestra.* [Emphasis added.] It is not enough that he should be able to represent his ideal conceptions of works unambiguously and with infectious intensity: he must add to this capacity that of leading the orchestra so as, in the course of playing, forthwith to correct faults, to help through special difficulties, to adjust the balance in advance—in short to establish a reciprocal relationship between conception and actual performance.[8]

In short, the acquisition and constant perfecting of a clear and highly meaningful conducting technique is the first order of business for the beginning conductor. The conductor possessing such a technique will receive the attention of his players without the constant urgings to "watch the beat." As Berlioz stated, *"An orchestra which does not watch the conductor's baton has no conductor."*[9]

If the conductor's technique is effective and efficient, he will spare himself the possibility of severe physical fatigue and even bursitis. The author, a number of years ago, was conducting two different orchestras during the same week plus an opera performance in a third location. His right shoulder was aching like an abscessed tooth. Another conductor—one with a very clear and precise technique—observed a rehearsal and pointed out that an unusual jerk preceded the second beat of a two-beat pattern. He showed us the fault and how to correct it quickly. An hour's practice of the improved pattern and the "toothache in the shoulder" disappeared. Since that evening, the thought of returning to the first pattern is accompanied only by remembrances of pain. Let the reader be reminded, however, that without the practice to make the new pattern part and parcel of our technique, habit would have allowed a reversion to the old pattern once more with its incumbent fatigue and shoulder distress.

PSYCHOLOGY OF CONDUCTING GESTURES

The books devoted to the art and craft of conducting rightfully devote much of their space to conducting technique and its acquisition. Little is mentioned of some of the psychological ramifications of certain gestures used by conductors.

All too often, concert-goers innocent of any knowledge of conducting technique tend to confuse gymnastics with conducting. Richard Strauss once observed that "you should not perspire when conducting; only the audience should get warm."[10] The more movement on the part of the conductor, the more difficult it is for the players to keep him in focus at the same time they are looking at the pages in front of them.

Certain gestures on the part of the conductors can be confusing for the players. A sudden thrust at a wind or brass player, for example, can cause the player to back away inadvertently, since on first blush, the motion might seem like a potential attack at his mouthpiece.

Any gesture which moves from the conductor straight at a player is confusing since its stopping point is very difficult to determine. Likewise, the picturesque traffic-policemen "stop" hand signal often used to acquire a reduction of sound might well have the effect of "stopping" the music rather than reducing the dynamic.

In much the same vein, the thrusted palm down signal for "softer" might have an adverse psychological effect on one or more players because of a possible "put down" connotation.

In more general terms, sudden angular movements may have a psychological effect of anger, an effect which no conductor obviously means. Even for more passionate and often violent outbursts of sound intended by the composer, the less angular movements on the part of the conductor will have a far better effect on both the music and the players.

The novice conductor would do well to analyze his gestures with the aid of a mirror to determine exactly what the possible reactions to a specific gesture might be. Practicing conducting with a mirror has been the object of some disagreement; an alternative is the video-taping of part of a rehearsal. By this means, the conductor can view himself as others see him and often overcome the use of certain types of gestures which might have adverse psychological effects on the players.

Samuel Krachmalnick, former Director of Symphony and Opera at the University of Washington, has often observed in his conducting classes, "Let the gesture bring the sound, not the sound the gesture." Recollection of this very wise observation should be coupled with constant vigilance on the part of the conductor to make every gesture absolutely clear, unequivocal, and not open to adverse psychological reactions.

"LET THE GESTURE BRING THE SOUND"

That the setting of tempo is perhaps the most important single function of the conductor can be deduced from the many references to this subject in the literature on conducting. Richard Wagner summed up the importance of tempo-setting with perhaps more eloquence than succinctness:

The right comprehension of the melos is the sole guide to the right tempo; these two things are inseparable. The one implies and qualifies the other.

The conductor's choice of tempo will show whether he understands the piece or not. With good players the true tempo induces correct phrasing and expression, and, conversely, with a conductor an idea of appropriate phrasing and expression will induce the conception of the true tempo.

I am persistently returning to the question of tempo because this is the point at which it becomes evident whether a conductor understands his business or not.[11]

Wagner's aesthetically correct statement does, however, need some further technical amplification: the correct tempo which comes from a proper understanding of the "melos," to use Wagner's term, must be properly prepared.

Wilhelm Fürtwangler perhaps best stated the concept of preparation which, while not always explicitly stated by the great conductors past and present, is nevertheless implicitly understood by them:

But, and this is the practical problem of all conducting, this point, this precision, cannot be attained with an orchestra when one makes such a point in the air, because what induces a group of people to come in at the same moment needs a certain optical preparation. It is not the movement of the down-beat itself, nor the accuracy and sharpness with which this down-beat is given, which determines the precision achieved by the orchestra, but the preparation which the conductor gives to this down-beat.[12]

What is needed by the conductor is an accurate concept of how the piece is to go before it starts. Leonard Bernstein once stated, "The chief element in the conductor's technique of communication is the preparation. Everything must be shown to the orchestra *before* it happens. Once the player is playing the note, it is too late."[13]

Some novice conductors may not have a real idea as to a method of acquiring the correct "melos" of the work before them. As a very practical suggestion, we urge that the conductor's "time at the desk," that is, his private study before facing the orchestra, be given over to actually singing the melody aloud while practicing his arm movements. Following such practice, it then becomes possible to "sing ahead" of the orchestra silently so that the preparatory gesture is indeed "in tempo." Hermann Scherchen once observed that "of all the human means of musical expression, singing is the most living or vital. Singing comes from within ourselves. The conductor's conception of a work should be a perfect inward singing.''[14] Such a vocal approach to strictly instrumental music can go far toward achieving Hindemith's ideal that *"no tempo should be so slow as to make it difficult for a melody to be recognizable, and no tempo so fast as to make a melody unrecognizable."*[15] Felix Weingartner once made the same point a bit differently when he said, "no slow tempo must be so slow that the melody of the piece is *not yet* recognizable, and no fast tempo so fast that the melody is *no longer* recognizable."[16]

CONDUCTING FROM MEMORY

The cult of the virtuoso spawned during the nineteenth century has led to many abuses, not the least of which is the fad of conducting from memory. True, certain conductors do possess a remarkable facility for memorizing, both visually and aurally. But the tyro is well advised to eschew this practice. Toscanini, suffering from severe myopia, did well to conduct without a score; but this is no adequate reason for his becoming a model for the many young conductors who feel they must do likewise.

Weingartner once said, "a conductor may really know a work by heart and yet fear that his memory may play him a trick, either through pardonable excitement or some other disturbing influence. In such cases it is always better to use the score; the audience is there to enjoy the work, not to admire the memory of the conductor."[17] And the late Pablo Casals, in answer to a question about his not conducting from memory replied, "I do not see the use of useless accomplishments. Richter was of the same mind."[18]

To memorize a score to be able to conduct it without reference to the printed page during performance requires, at least for most of us, a fantastic amount of time. If the admonitions of Casals, Richter, and Weingartner are of any value, they should be heeded, particularly by the conductors of orchestras that are in need of the conductor's help at all times.

The argument for conducting from memory goes somewhat like "the conductor should have the score in his head, not his head in the score." To be sure, there is merit in looking at players, and it can be done with perhaps a more casual reference to the printed page at the time of performance. We remember a performance by one of the great orchestras where the conductor, performing a difficult program from memory, never looked at the orchestra, only at the floor of the podium as though the score were there. One almost expected him to reach for his shoes to turn the pages. Young conductors, desiring to emulate a Toscanini or other great conductor, should perhaps strive first to acquire their understanding of the music, rather than their prowess of memory.

THE CONDUCTOR AS TEACHER

Enjoyment of any art form increases understanding. The community orchestra exists as much for the benefit of the players as for anyone. The enjoyment of their participation in the orchestra will increase as their understanding increases. With this in mind, it is obvious that the conductor of such an orchestra is indeed a teacher.

> To develop a good amateur orchestra, the conductor must have had sufficient training and experience in the mechanics of his art to enable him to teach his players, collectively and individually, to realize to the fullest their potentialities of the moment. The key word in the preceding sentence is "teach." The conductor of an amateur group must be a teacher in the finest sense of the word, for the material with which he has to work is seldom expert enough to produce the desired musical effects without detailed technical advice.[19]

In this context, the young conductor should be careful not to confuse "teaching" with "lecturing." Let it be understood by the community orchestra conductor that the most effective form of teaching is the conductor himself displaying (not always verbally) a sound *musical* understanding of what he is about. Elements of various musical styles are imparted to the players with the view toward increasing the players' understanding, hence enjoyment of what they are about. The conductor's role as teacher is, in many respects, a "quiet" one. It is here that the leadership of the conductor can be the most effective.

If the conductor acquires the ability to impart to his players the same kinds of understanding about the music as were imparted to him by his most effective teachers, then his teaching role is fulfilled. We must reiterate that this teaching is not done through lecturing, but through the quiet imparting of the best musical ideals which the conductor possesses.

SOME OTHER REQUIREMENTS

The conductor should have spent time playing in an orchestra to gain the insight of the orchestral player. The late Pierre Monteux once remarked to the author that he had started his career in Paris as a violinist, later switching to the viola so he could spend more time watching conductors. It was Arturo Toscanini, the orchestral cellist, who sprang into the breach when the regular conductor was unavailable, thus launching his long and successful career on the podium. The actual experience of playing in an orchestra is invaluable for conductor training.

Lloyd Pfautsch has made the same point for choral conductors in very lucid terms:

> It is most important that the background of every choral conductor include the regimen of singing in a choral ensemble. In no other way can he appreciate the significance of individual contribution to the ensemble sound, individual responsibility in following the conductor's directions, and individual reaction to different rehearsal procedures. Without this experience, a choral conductor will lack empathetic understanding of the individual and the group.[20]

Each point advanced by Pfautsch applies equally to the orchestral conductor. Orchestra players are humans, not automatons. They inevitably react to what the conductor says, and what he does, and how he gestures. Indeed, they react to his mere presence in the rehearsal room and to his first steps onto the podium at a concert. The conductor as a person—or as a personality, if you will—is under constant observation by many pairs of human eyes and ears. He would do well, when he practices in front of his mirror, to abandon the role of Narcissus and learn to see himself as *others* see him. If he has served an apprenticeship as an "observer" in the orchestra, he will be in a better position to appreciate these human relationships empathetically.

The conductor should also have considerable facility at the keyboard, most necessarily if he has inclinations toward conducting opera. The best conductors are not necessarily piano virtuosi, but keyboard ability is a very important part of the conductor's training.

To be a successful operatic conductor, one must have served an apprenticeship as accompanist and vocal coach. The opera conductor who does not fully comprehend all that is involved in singing would be in much the same position as a football coach who is ignorant of the techniques of blocking and tackling. The community orchestra conductor will inevitably be drawn into some form of musical theater direction and will be in a much stronger position to help such productions if he can give keyboard assistance to the singers. This is not to say that non-pianists cannot become conductors, but those conductors who have considerable keyboard skill tend to become better conductors.

In addition to assisting singers who may be appearing with the orchestra, some keyboard facility can help in the approach to more contemporary music. Daniel Moe, choral conductor and composer, has suggested that "It may be worth noting that a conductor who is quite capable of approaching a Mozart, Beethoven, or Brahms score without reference to the keyboard may not be able to do so with a modern score. The conductor must be absolutely secure in his understanding of the various pitch relationships before he enters the rehearsal.''[21]

It more or less goes without saying that a conductor's other areas of knowledge must also include a strong grasp of music theory and history, orchestration (including the ability to transpose rapidly), the ability to read in all clefs normally found in orchestra scores, and a sense of stylistic "correctness" for all periods and styles of music.

The conductor will perhaps not have had the time to learn all of the above and acquire the skills of a practicing psychologist as well. Yet human relations are terribly important for the conductor, and must not be overlooked. The late Sir John Barbirolli once observed:

> The success with which the conductor inspires eagerness and willingness in the men of the orchestra (who must follow him anyway) determines the conductor's powers. The happiest relationship results when the conductor regards the men, not as employees to whom he has a right to dictate, but as co-workers, with whom he comes together for the common purpose of joyous music making. The men should be willing to follow him, not through fear or duty, but through affection and respect.''[22]

If Barbirolli's convictions applied to paid professional orchestras, it seems all the more incumbent upon the community orchestra conductor to heed his advice where the players are involved because they *want* to be and not because they are paid for it.

Orchestras may forgive a slip in technique now and then, but bad manners or tyrannical behavior will earn for the conductor only disdain. Making music with an orchestra is a cooperative effort between conductor and players; the conductor whose attitude breathes cooperation will get the most from his players.

The conductor should strive to broaden his intellect in other areas besides music. To quote Lloyd Pfautsch once more:

> Exposure to the creative efforts of a dramatist, novelist, poet, painter, sculptor, or choreographer can enhance artistic sensibility. Opening one's mind to the thinking of philosophers, theologians, politicians, scientists, economists, and so on, can contribute a breadth of knowledge which not only suggests a more complete human being but also helps the choral (or orchestral) conductor relate more effectively to the other human beings with whom and for whom he works. This openmindedness also encourages learning from the other disciplines as well as willingness to change, to experiment, to adopt, and to appropriate.[23]

Music was not created in a vacuum. Mozart, Beethoven, Wagner and all other great composers were vitally alive to other things going on about them. If the music of past and present was *created* within the mainstream of all human thought and endeavor of the time, it behooves the *re-creators* of that music to re-create it within the mainstream of human thought and endeavor of their own time.

Conductors should certainly learn from the examples of their colleagues. There is much to be gained from conversations at conferences and conventions, as well as from visiting other conductors' rehearsals if at all possible. In this connection, the author has never ceased to wonder at the callous indifference displayed by so-called conducting students in an academic situation he has observed. When the conducting class was over, they never bothered to attend the orchestral rehearsals which in this case *immediately followed* the conducting class! Apparently they assumed that all of the art and craft of conducting could be learned by enrolling in a class. D. E. Inghelbrecht has pointed out clearly the fallacy of such assumptions: "In our haste, young musisians no longer think of finding the best tuition by attending rehearsals of great conductors. Here alone is it possible to appreciate the real value of conductors, less by looking at them than by listening to their remarks and demands."[24] While Inghelbrecht was writing of a time in Paris when the great conductors were constant visitors, his remarks are still valid for the younger conductors who are more isolated. The conductors one chooses to observe need not all be "great" ones, for much can be learned (or unlearned?) from more obscure conductors as well. The author has perhaps benefited as much from "negative" learning (what *not* to do) in watching conductors of very modest talents as he has from the "positive" influence of the very gifted ones.

The author was fortunate during his early years to study conducting under the tutelege of the late Pierre Monteux. In the many intervening years, the question of "What did you learn?" was always answered, "Hopefully, humility before the composer." Leonard Bernstein remarked in like manner,

> Well, there is our ideal conductor. And perhaps the chief requirement of all is that he be humble before the composer; that he never interpose himself between the music and the audience; that all his efforts, however strenuous or glamorous, be made in the service of the composer's meaning—the music itself, which, after all, is the whole reason for the conductor's existence.[25]

Father William Finn, himself a distinguished choral conductor, stated, "Fidelity to a composer's intentions, as far as they may be discerned, is the cornerstone of music ethics."[26] And Erwin Stein, conductor and critic, wrote, "When all has been said, the truth remains that musical performance is less a matter of historical faithfulness, than of artistic sincerity."[27]

ADVANCED TRAINING OPPORTUNITIES

For the young conductor who has finished formal degree work, but who wants to pursue additional study, there are several ways in which this can be accomplished. It is unfortunate that most of these can be costly in terms of time and money as well as time away from one's own orchestra.

Each summer, the American Symphony Orchestra League operates an Institute of Orchestral Studies at Orkney Springs, Virginia. This institute, under the artistic direction of Richard Lert, is open to conductors by audition. In addition to working under the supervision of Dr. Lert and his assistants, there are orchestral concerts, conducted by both professional conductors and those in training, under the auspices of the Shenandoah Music Festival.

The Domaine School in Hancock, Maine, founded by the late Pierre Monteux, is another training possibility. The school operates for approximately one month during the summer. There have been a distinguished number of conductors now working with our larger orchestras who have received much of their training at the Domaine School.

Conducting competitions are another route in receiving some advanced training as well as competing for prizes. Most notable are those sponsored by the Baltimore and Oakland Symphony orchestras. In addition to these within the United States, there are several competitions held abroad. Unfortunately, with the exception of the Oakland competition, there is an age limitation which limits many applicants.

Two new developments which have yet to be made completely final are being planned by the Conductor's Guild of the American Symphony Orchestra League. The first of these is a series of three conductors' workshops which will be held in conjunction with the regional workshops of the League. These will feature a master conductor, an orchestra, and conducting opportunities. Applicants will be screened by audition, and the finalists will be chosen by the teaching staff. Although of short duration, these workshops will be a valuable aid for the younger conductor wishing to receive additional training under the tutelage of an experienced master teacher.

Somewhat further from fruition is the development of an American Conducting Academy. Although the realization of the academy awaits funding, the concept is for the applicant who passes an audition to work for up to six or eight weeks with a master teacher and orchestra.

In the ease of both the conductors' workshops and the American Conducting Academy, there will be no age limitations.

SUMMARY

In the age of specialization in which we live, it is almost paradoxical that the conductor must be not only a musical "jack of all trades," but an understanding psychologist, father-confessor, and social worker as well. Beyond these "generalist" requirements, he must hone his conducting technique to a degree of effectiveness that will make his musical intentions unmistakably clear, polish his keyboard skills, and strive for a degree of humility before the composers whose music he re-creates— almost impossible in perhaps the most non-humble of musical professions.

Integrity, no less than humility, is a virtue essential for the conductor even more than for all other interpreters. It is not unusual for youth to be poorly endowed with it, but it is tragic not to achieve it at a riper age. Often modesty enhances a conductor's merit, his real merit and not that which he gets from the untrustworthy popularity of snobs.[28]

chapter 5

Some Rehearsal Procedures

The conductor and his orchestra must now face the first rehearsal. For the younger conductor, this can be an almost traumatic experience, for it is in this first rehearsal that conductor and orchestra initiate their musical acquaintance. All too often, mutual reactions at the beginning can bode good or ill for many rehearsals to come. If the conductor is to assume the role of leader in the orchestra's undertakings, he must take care to insure a favorable working relationship from the very start.

AUDITIONING PLAYERS

Even before the first rehearsal, it may be desirable to audition some, if not most, of the players. This will give the conductor an opportunity to meet and deal with each individual as a person, and to assess his or her capabilities and potential. With community orchestras the matter of auditions can be very sensitive. Many adult instrumentalists, particularly those whose instruments have lain dormant for some time, are understandably reluctant to play alone in front of anyone. This seems to be more true of string players than of wind and brass players.

The conductor will probably want to audition, and decide in advance, a few key string positions such as section principals, taking care to insure that players who may have held such positions previously do not have their feelings hurt. If there is a good turnout of string players, one can save both time and embarrassment all around by adopting the following effective expedient: at the rehearsal, divide the violinists equally among first and second violin parts, then exchange parts for the second half of the rehearsal. As time goes on, by judicious shifting around, the conductor can maneuver the players into their most effective positions.

> The system of placing the best violins in the first section has one
> other major fault: it places the more competent players en masse in
> in the first violin section, while the unfortunate remainder wind up
> across the railroad tracks as second. Here they proceed to bog down
> in a mass inferiority complex of tremendous proportions. It is this
> sort of procedure which has given rise to the artificial stigma, both
> musical and social, now attached to the words "second violin."[1]

Such comments as: "Why don't we try such-and-such seating arrangement to see if we get better balance," or "We need more strength in the
second violins, and for this rehearsal let's try you, you, and you playing
second for the time being," avoids "locking-in" certain players in some
sections (at least in their minds), and gives some flexibility to the group
as well as creating a potentially more cooperative atmosphere. The conductor must keep reassuring the second violins of their importance, and
he should find ways to let them have some of the limelight usually ac-
corded to the first violins and solo wind and brass players.

In this country, where solo and ensemble contest for high school students has existed for many years, even adult wind and brass players are
somewhat less reluctant than their string counterparts to play alone. Since
there are often more applicants than players for the wind and brass sections (there are never enough violinists!), auditions should always be
held away from the rest of the orchestra. The present writer was asked to
audition for a community orchestra trumpet section many years ago in
full view of the rest of the orchestra. Although he passed the audition
and was accepted into the orchestra, the experience was somewhat un-
nerving. It is better for the conductor alone to do the auditioning. After
all, the player has been in a one-to-one relationship with a teacher for
many years; it is a psychological hurdle—almost a traumatic experience
for some—suddenly to have to play before a committee, no matter how
understanding and informal they try to be.

Audition material varies with the experience and background of the
players. A prepared list of excerpts from which to draw, including sight-
reading material, given out in advance, will help: the players then know
beforehand what the requirements are. In the case of a new group, however, this is not always practical. A solo or excerpt of the player's choice
will at least provide the advantage of starting from a known point of
reference. For sight-reading material, the choice is greater and more
difficult to select fairly. Appendix B lists several suggestions for audition
material for each instrument of the orchestra.

During the 1972-73 season, three major symphony orchestras had
violin openings all requiring the first violin part of Strauss' *Don Juan*
as an auditioning excerpt. This makes little or no sense for the community orchestra unless *Don Juan* is in the conductor's mind for a future

program. In most community orchestras, given the extraordinary difficulties of the string writing in the opening measures alone, that work should *not* be in the conductor's mind for programming!

The sight-reading material used at auditions should be drawn from whatever repertoire has a reasonable chance of appearing on the programs. The player should be able to cope with moderately intricate rhythmic patterns, some degree of chromaticism, a variety of dynamic possibilities, and have the ability to maintain a steady metrical pulse. Excerpts full of a variety of musical snares should be avoided, since, in the community orchestra, one expects the player to enjoy what he or she is playing. "The object is not to trip the candidate, but to find out how well he can handle music of the difficulty he will encounter during his membership."[2]

If it appears that auditions are going to cause more problems than solutions (and often this can be determined by a few well-timed questions), it is wise to avoid them until the atmosphere within the orchestra is more favorable for auditions. Within the context of auditions, the conductor must bear in mind that in a community orchestra the players are there because they wish to make music together—not to serve as the conductor's "trained seals."

SOME SUGGESTED REHEARSAL GUIDELINES

The following suggestions are arranged more or less in order of importance. Due to the special nature of the community orchestra, some things are bound to arise during rehearsals which would not ordinarily occur in a more professional situation and they must be dealt with.

The conductor *must* be sure that the rehearsal letters or numbers in the parts coincide with those of the score. Much rehearsal time is wasted if these insignificant landmarks are overlooked. A few minutes with the parts *before* they go on the stands can save many precious minutes of rehearsal time. When stopping to make a correction, or to go back over a rough place, the conductor will save time by saying, "Before F (pause), nine measures" rather than saying, "Nine measures (pause), before F"; in the latter instance, it might well be nine measures before any other letter. The pause gives the players time to find "F" first, then count the number of measures. Give the primary location, "F," first, then the number of measures before or after. If the parts have no letters or measure numbers, put them in *before* the first rehearsal! Should letters or numbers disagree between parts and score, transfer the letters from the parts into the score.

For conductors without string backgrounds, the question of bowings can be both perplexing and frustrating. If the conductor has good section leaders, they can be entrusted to take care of the bowings. The section leaders are often willing to meet with the conductor before the parts go to the players; bowing can then be discussed so as to create more or less uniform bowings for the piece to be played. In most community orchestras, many of the string players are not equal to some of the bowings suggested by the more virtuoso players in the section. Some attempt should be made to establish bowings that all of the players can realize. Sometimes bowings first suggested by the section leaders may be overruled by the conductor if there is a good reason. If he has in mind a particular effect for a certain passage, and that effect depends upon the bowings, the section leaders may be prevailed upon to accept the conductor's intentions.

Many conductors have not found a perfect solution to the problem of making corrections, particularly when a mistake is made by a solo player. If the player is of high calibre, he or she knows the instant a mistake is made and no mention of it should come from the podium; a "knowing glance" from the conductor is all that is necessary. If, in rehearsing the passage in question, the mistake occurs again, simply ask to see the part or ask the player to read back the notes. Orchestra parts are often in error and the player may well be playing what is written.

As a general rule, it is not a good idea to mention an offending player by name; rather, make the correction by instrument, "second oboe, is the sharp sign omitted before the 'F'?" On the other hand, if a solo player has played a passage particularly well, then compliment him by name. In the case of errors within a section, call it to the attention of the entire section even though it might be highly obvious which player made the mistake. If that individual shows by his or her reaction that he was the offender, no comment is necessary.

Many conductors sit during rehearsals and stand, of course, during concerts (unless physically handicapped). It would be far better for the conductor always to stand. The shape and size of the beat patterns, as well as the beat level, is considerably different between standing and sitting positions. Players accustomed to one frame of reference in rehearsals who are suddenly confronted with something else at the concert may be led into confusion. Further, from the sheer physical point of view, severe cases of bursitis, not to mention tired back muscles, can result from conducting from a seated position.

The time of the week when rehearsals are held should be carefully thought out in advance of the first rehearsal. Since orchestra players are often found in church choirs, for example, orchestra rehearsals must be held on a different night if at all possible. In most communities, the majority of choir rehearsals are on the same night, so it is possible to avoid this problem Not all conflicts in a community can be avoided, but careful planning can eliminate most of them.

The rehearsal may start a bit late from time to time due to traffic congestions, weather, or parking problems; but the rehearsal *must never* go overtime unless the conductor has warned the orchestra beforehand. Of course; one must not let tardy rehearsal beginnings become a habit. But on-time conclusions of rehearsals tend to encourage punctual beginnings.

The break in a rehearsal has become an established custom in most orchestra. This is a good time for the conductor to confer with principal players, double check for possible errors in the parts, and attend to other such time-consuming tasks. At the same time, it gives the players a chance to relax and visit. If the orchestra has an established Women's Committee, light refreshments could be provided from time to time during the break; this should not become a habit at *every* rehearsal, for it does create a burden upon those serving the refreshments and there is a danger of the break getting longer and longer!

The break is also a good time, if advisable or necessary, to dismiss part of the orchestra and hold sectional rehearsals. Unless an entire rehearsal is devoted to a string rehearsal, for instance, it is best to have the full orchestra present at the beginning of the rehearsal to work on those selections that use the whole orchestra. Then players who are no longer needed may be dismissed early. Some conductors make the mistake of asking certain players to come at midpoint in the rehearsal: it is unlikely that they will all arrive together. The orchestra is accustomed to starting at a fixed time, and asking them to come at a different hour, unless very unusual circumstances prevail, can create problems.

As regards the conductor's rehearsal attire: long-sleeved, dark-colored shirts or jackets serve rehearsal purposes best. The conductor's bare arms can be distracting to the players, and since most batons are either white or natural wood color, a dark background provides the best illumination for the beat. If the conductor must wear glasses, they should have either very dark, heavy frames, or light wire frames which make them almost invisible. Heavy, dark frames tend to focus attention on the conductor's eyes when eye contact is very important. Perhaps contact lenses would be even better.

Podium height and baton length depend solely on the conductor's build: the shorter the conductor, the higher the podium and longer the baton. Podiums should not be so high that players sitting in the front must strain their necks looking up at the conductor, but high enough so that the woodwind and brass players can see him as well.

Batons, particularly if they are long, must be stiff enough so that they do not give a whip effect in rapid motion or quiver with apprehension in slower motions.

The conductor must avoid excessive talking. Players with the music before them are not usually interested in long analytical lectures or prior personal experiences, they are more interested in the music itself than in the conductor's prattle. Dr. Stanley Chapple once remarked to a student conductor, "Conduct with your stick, not with your mouth."

There will be many times when explanatory remarks are needed. For the community orchestra where a number of younger players are necessarily present, certain unfamiliar terminology may need clearing up. This is not to suggest that the conductor deliver himself of long, pretentious musicological lectures, but his explanations must be clear and very much to the point.

Very often it is helpful to have the section leaders demonstrate specific solutions, e.g., certain types of bowings or correct ways of executing "ponticello" or "sul tasto" directions. Likewise, it can help if string section leaders insure that all members of the section have mutes when called for.

Rehearsal tempos vary from conductor to conductor. The author's experience has suggested that the first reading be more or less in the performance tempo, accomplishing two objectives: giving the players a fair concept of what the final tempo will be, and giving the conductor and players an idea of where the truly nasty places within a work are.

Working out these nasty places in rehearsal can be either very enlightening or very frustrating to both players and conductor. Some spots which, in the score, appear to present problems, may actually be taken in stride once the players "have at them." The conductor should be cautious about slowing down the tempo too much in order to work out difficult places. True, the players have to see what the notes are, and plan and adjust their fingerings. But, rather typically, the natural flow of the music is its own best aid to execution. This is true where the composer has written competently for strings or for wind instruments. And it is hoped that the conductor will execute music that has been competently written.

It is helpful to work out similar passages at the same time, as for example, a difficult *stretto* that appears in the exposition and reappears in the recapitulation. Or there may be several chromatic transitions at various places in a piece, in which case one would deal with these altogether in order to learn how to solve this particular problem. This process of isolating similar passages has the further advantage of providing players an insight into the form and structure of the work being rehearsed. And this without the conductor having to go into a windy explanation of form.

Much the same process can aid the articulation of fugal sections. Different sections of the orchestra will sooner or later get a chance at the fugue subject. Those who have entries on the same pitches can even rehearse the subject all together for consistency in phrasing, dynamics, and so on. Or where the answer differs from the subject, or the subject enters in different keys, separate rehearsal of these places will provide a firm grasp of the skeletal framework of the fugue. Such "selective" working out of crucial thematic material will in the end conserve much valuable rehearsal time.

Never stop the players without giving a reason audibly to the players. The author vividly recalls a case in point: at his summer camp for conductors, the late Pierre Monteux was quietly watching one of his young conductors at work with the orchestra. The conductor stopped, had the orchestra repeat, and stopped again. The music sounded the same each time. Finally, Monteux, with great exasperation asked why the conductor had stopped. He had neglected to tell the players what was wrong and how to correct it.

There is far more to being a good rehearsal conductor than merely detecting errors. For every stoppage there must be a reason given. The only way the players can correct a mistake, unless a highly obvious one, is to be told what to change. Such corrections must *always* be administered with much gentleness! The object is to encourage good musicianship, not the "heel" and "lie down" of the training kennel.

Much can be accomplished in difficult rehearsals if the conductor is able to pace the rehearsal so as to obtain the maximum results with the minimum of time. Constant rehearsing and re-rehearsing of the same troublesome place can create ever-increasing tensions in the orchestra and the possibility of compounding mistakes. A change of pace, a word of humor or a suggestion that "this passage is to take home and practice on your own," and then going on to another place or another composition, will go a long way toward reducing rehearsal tensions.

A bit of humor now and then can be very helpful providing it is injected discreetly and not overdone. The conductor must remember that he is there to conduct, not to be a comedian. Individual members of the orchestra must *never* be the brunt of any joke, no matter how innocent. Humor is best used if it can fit the specific situation of the moment. Random jokes or anecdotes unrelated to what is happening in the rehearsal break the attention of the players and waste time.

Perhaps the most important word in the conductor's rehearsal vocabulary is "please." This word, used liberally, will go a long way toward insuring player cooperation. Likewise, many "thank yous" during the rehearsal will let the players know that the conductor appreciates their effort. The author has found that more rehearsal flies are caught with sugar ("please") than with vinegar ("do it!").

When asking for a certain response during rehearsals, the conductor would do well to phrase the request in such a manner as "Please, Beethoven would like you to do it this way," rather than, "I want it played this way.'' Such an approach tends to lessen the impression that the conductor is a dictator. This kind of request increases cooperation, which is really the name of the game in any orchestra, community or professional.

We have mentioned the use of videotape and recordings for rehearsals in a previous chapter. The usefulness of these devices as a possible incentive to the players must be strictly weighed against the loss of rehearsal time involved in a playback. And let us not forget: rehearsal time is a commodity in very short supply; the conductor must use it in the most responsible way.

For many reasons, conductors have historically been reluctant to open rehearsals to visitors. While some defense of this reluctance can be made on the part of professional orchestras, the same posture is indefensible for the community orchestra. There will be times when members of the board are interested in how the orchestra is progressing, or members of the press would like to drop in. Interested students also might like to see what makes an orchestra ''tick.'' We pointed out in an earlier chapter that the community orchestra's success depends on community support. ''Open'' rehearsals can help cultivate this community support. During the author's tenure as conductor of the Port Angeles Symphony, he issued an invitation annually to the community at large and more often to members of the board and younger music students in the community to visit rehearsals. The response was not widespread, but no one in the community ever felt that they had been shut out.

Discipline in the orchestra must come from the conductor. If a proper rehearsal attitude emanates from the podium, it will in most cases pervade the entire orchestra. If the conductor is habitually late to rehearsals, the players will be late. If the conductor's own preparation of the scores is slipshod, the orchestra will be less likely to practice at home on their own. Talking in one section while another section is rehearsing a difficult passage cannot be tolerated; a gentle reprimand from the conductor usually solves the problem. If a single player seems to be a constant offender, the conductor should speak to him privately.

In orchestras where there are both adults and young people, a greater discipline problem is posed. If the conductor can communicate to the younger members of the orchestra that it is an honor to be playing with adults, it usually ends many of the discipline problems within a mixed-age orchestra.

Unfortunately, the term ''artistic temperament'' has been used as a euphemism for impoliteness and bad manners. Genuine artistic temperament is another matter: it is a fine-tuned sensitivity for nuances of good taste and style both in overall conception and in details of musical interpretation. This ideal is difficult enough to achieve without the distractions of boorishness. The community orchestra has to be a labor of love on the part of all concerned. The conductor may growl and scold at his wife and kids at home, if they will put up with it. But the moment he enters the rehearsal hall, the rule should be courtesy and politeness to the players at all times, even in the midst of frustrating difficulties. Firmness, yes. Dedication to musical principles, yes. But it is *calmness*, combined with authority, that achieves musical results beyond expectations. Remember that if you have to "blow up" and lose control, *you are no longer master of the situation.* "Self control comes first; then control over others."[3]

Lest the conductor, after several very frustrating and possibly unprofitable rehearsals, become overwhelmed with the hopelessness of producing a successful concert, let us point out the phenomenon well known to more experienced community orchestra conductors: "the adrenalin syndrome." It has been our experience, time and again, that no matter how badly the rehearsals have gone, somehow the orchestra pulls most of it together at the concert. This is not to say that things do not go wrong in concerts. But we have found that most of the time things go much better than we often have any right to expect.

The players take great pride in their orchestra and want it to sound well in front of the public. The pressure of performance—concert nerves and all!—most often brings out the best. Obviously, this does not mean that the conductor can relax at rehearsals, for no surge of adrenalin ever pulled a badly prepared concert together. But if the players have become *aware* of the problems during rehearsal, there is every chance that this rather standard kind of miracle will save the concert. Let this dissuade the less-experienced conductor, distraught over seemingly disastrous rehearsals, from slashing his wrists on the eve of the concert!

SUMMARY

The foregoing suggestions are not a precise blueprint to successful rehearsals, but are the result of years rehearsing the author's own orchestra as well as numerous guest conducting appearances. Perhaps the one most important suggestion is that the conductor should treat each and every one of his players as a human being, and consider himself as the servant of the composer.

chapter 6

General Program Considerations

The late Dr. Fritz Reiner once eloquently remarked, "I spend 80 per cent of my time in planning programs, the other 20 per cent in transferring my ideas to the musicians."[1] If a conductor of his stature and ability spent that amount of time planning his programs, it behooves the conductor of a community orchestra to give at least equal time to his own planning.

GENERAL CONSIDERATIONS

A conductor new to a community must first undertake to determine the musical tastes and attitudes of his community. This can be accomplished through a variety of methods, the *least* effective of which is by verbal inquiry.

A rewarding procedure is to examine the record collections of people in whose homes he visits—particularly board members. This can be done discreetly and will provide far more valuable information than direct questioning. A comment or question about one or two recorded works in a library will usually provoke much informative discussion.

The local record store(s) and public library circulation desk are additional sources of information. The recorded works most often purchased or borrowed tells much about the musical attitude of a community.

Armed with such information, the conductor should allow some common sense to prevail in planning his programs. Size and instrumentation of his orchestra and kinds of programs previously played (if any), together with the conductor's own preferences, should guide program content.

The conductor who blends his own musical tastes with those of his community will shape the tastes of his community toward an increasingly higher caliber of musical fare. Program planning must be done with the same care with which a dietician plans meals.

One of the techniques with community orchestras which the author has found to be quite successful is asking the orchestra members for program suggestions for subsequent seasons. Very often the suggested works are not possible because of difficulty or unavailability of the performance materials, but being asked does give the players the feeling that their preferences are being given consideration. If the conductor cannot program a player's suggestion, it is helpful to explain the reasons to him. This is another means of cementing relations with the players who are playing because they really want to.

Programs should be well balanced in terms of the great historical periods in music. Many pre-Romantic works do not use full winds and brass, but they deserve hearing as well as those pieces that use the full orchestra. Including a Bach concerto or suite or a Mozart or Haydn symphony will provide program variety and if the heavy-brass section complains that it does not have enough to do, beginning the concert with a *Turmsonate* of Petzel or the "Fanfare" from Dukas' *La Peri* will provide the audience with a new sample of the panorama of music while focusing attention on the brass.

A more subtle and often overlooked danger is that of creating what the late Pierre Monteux once referred to as "key monotony."[2] In a program that leans heavily to the Classical period, where the tonal centers remain closely related, one must insure some variety in key centers even though the chord progressions are similar. This can be accomplished by separating works in the same or closely related keys by means of works in more remote tonalities. An audience, without realizing why, can become bored with seemingly endless reiterations of dominant-tonic progressions in closely related keys.

Tonal colors can become monotonous as well. Haydn, Mozart, Schubert, and early Beethoven utilized essentially the same instrumental combinations; although the music is different, the "classical sound" pervades all four. Therefore, it is wise to include not more than two of these composers on any program unless one is planning a one-composer concert. In the same vein, if an orchestra is fortunate enough to be able to perform a Mahler symphony, it would be wise not to precede it with a Wagner overture.

Most orchestra programs lean heavily to music of central Europe; variety should be added by playing compositions from other areas to balance off the staple diet of Haydn-through-Brahms. Much interesting music comes from Spain, the Americas, Scandinavia, France, and England.

Conductors receive requests for specific works which are usually the large Romantic works in the standard repertoire. Many of these pieces have been recorded over and over again by the world's great orchestras; there will be inevitable comparisons between a local performance and the music lover's "favorite" recording. Where possible, select works that are less ambitious but *stylistically similar.* For example, Tchaikovsky's second ("Little Russian") and third ("Polish") symphonies have the Tchaikovsky "sound" but do not bristle with the difficulties of the last three symphonies. They will probably satisfy audience desire for this composer without the orchestra facing the hazards of comparison with the Philadelphia Orchestra. Moreover, the audience will have the pleasant experience of feeling like musicologists in "discovering" a little-known work of genuine merit. Further suggestions for substitutions will be given in a later chapter.

There is no harm in repeating works which have been well performed and well received in previous concerts. The same material should not be performed over and over, but certain pieces can and should be performed again, allowing some time to elapse in between. Too many conductors try to establish themselves by conducting as many works as possible. A more limited repertoire may enhance the musical growth of the community just as much as an extensive one and generally better performances result because of the residue of familiarity which remains over several years.

With a limited number of concerts each season, the conductor must program soloists' vehicles with the same care that he plans the orchestral repertoire. Where there is little live music other than the orchestra's, endless repetitions of the Tchaikovsky, Beethoven, and Mendelssohn concertos can do little to stimulate the growth of musical taste. In planning a season's programs, the conductor would do well first of all to include the concertos and arias he would like to present and then search for the soloists to perform them. In this way, variety can be "built in," whereas, if the soloists are contracted for first, they may insist upon bringing along their favorite war-horses and the conductor is locked into a situation he can no longer adequately control.

An endless succession of visiting pianists or violinists or singers leads to sterility in program content. It is a good practice to use at least one orchestra member as soloist each season. The programs of some orchestras suggest that the conductor has never heard of clarinet, trumpet, or horn concertos.

It is vital for the conductor to ascertain the musical climate and tastes of his community as soon as possible. He should then plan his programs to include a varied offering from the great historical periods of music, at the same time avoiding monotony in key centers, tonal colors, national origin of the music, and redundance in soloistic vehicles.

SOLOISTS AND THEIR TREATMENT

The engagement of "name" soloists should be given careful consideration by community orchestras. The cost of their fees—running from
several hundred to over two thousand dollars—should be weighed against
potential increase in box office receipts which the soloist might generate.
The growing number of highly gifted soloists on the faculties of colleges
and universities throughout the country is a relatively untapped source
of talent which smaller orchestras should investigate. In most cases their
fees are considerably less than those of the "name" artists, and their
schedules for rehearsals and performances more flexible.*

Conducting the orchestral accompaniment for concertos and arias
demands special skills more properly discussed under pre-rehearsal preparation. However, since beginning conductors rarely have experience in
this aspect of their craft, a few suggestions at this point may be helpful in
avoiding pitfalls, especially as there may be only one or two rehearsals
with the soloist before the concert.

If the orchestra engages a "name" artist, the conductor's preliminary
homework should consist of listening carefully to that artist's recording
of the programmed work, if one is available. If not available, then he
should listen to several recordings of the concerto, so that the variety of
possible interpretations can be studied. In most situations the soloist will
have only one rehearsal with the orchestra so a "talk-through" with the
soloist prior to the rehearsal is a must. The conductor can then mark his
score, thereby conserving rehearsal time with the soloist.

It is also helpful for the conductor to play through the solo part on the
piano to get the feel of the solo line, if he has sufficient keyboard ability.
Less experienced conductors often become so involved with purely orchestral passages that solo parts and their accompaniments are neglected.
The conductor should alert the orchestra (before the soloist is there) of
any possible excursions away from a strictly metrical reading of the notes.
Adequately learning the solo part helps the conductor "find" a soloist
should there be lapses of memory.**

A local soloist can usually be at several rehearsals, thereby providing

*Another source of soloist talent for very moderate fees is through the Leventritt Com-
petition. The Leventritt Foundation pays the difference between the artist's normal fee and
the modest fee assessed the sponsoring orchestra. Details are available from the Leventritt
Foundation, c/o Thea Dispeker Artists' Representative, 59 East 54th Street, New York,
New York 10022.

**The practice of a soloist playing from memory is only a recent innovation and no harm
results if the soloist uses music. Particularly in the case of smaller orchestras, where a certain amount of nervousness exists in both soloist and orchestra, or with inexperienced
soloists, smoother performances are often obtained with the soloist using the music.

more time to work out differences in interpretation. Many of the above comments are still valid, however, as they conserve rehearsal time.

Two social rather than musical considerations need to be mentioned in regard to soloists. Many communities still follow the custom of presenting flowers to a soloist, men as well as women. Corsages are cumbersome, especially if the soloist is a string player. Some flowers also produce allergic reactions for some persons, which must be avoided. It is well to discuss this in advance with the soloist.

Receptions and parties following performances can often be as tiring as the performance itself, and should be cleared with the soloist before the performance. Some artists' managers specify in their contracts the desires of the soloist in this regard.

Fortunately, there are few instances in a conductor's life when soloists become difficult. Soloists are, after all, people—some quiet and cooperative, others less so. In the case of a "problem" soloist, the best practice is to do whatever he or she wants, give the best possible accompaniment, and let the matter rest there. A reengagement need not follow!

In working with soloists, better performances result if the conductor knows the solo part well and if he and the orchestra make every effort to accommodate the artist in every possible way, both musically and socially.

PROGRAMMING CONTEMPORARY MUSIC

Special consideration must be given to contemporary music. New music must be included, but it must be acceptable to both the orchestra and the audience. The more avant-garde compositions usually will be accepted less quickly by players and listeners; the style is too "new" for the majority of both to grasp immediately. Further, the notation of much avant-garde music is so totally new to most orchestras that extra rehearsal time will be required. With the inadequate rehearsal time of most community orchestras, programming works with extra difficulties can detract from the performance of the entire program.

The conductor is in a better position to travel less-well-known avenues of contemporary musical expression if the community has a tradition for new things. However, it is far better to program new music bearing in mind the *present* aesthetic capacities of orchestra and public; later, one can gently nudge them down the path of progress.

Many compositions of Robert Ward, William Bergsma, Roy Harris, Aaron Copland, Alan Hovhaness, or Theron Kirk (to name a few from the vast list of American composers of the mid-twentieth century) can be performed by most community orchestras and will have much audience appeal. These compositions are not "watered-down," nor do they make concessions to popular taste. They are strong works which can hold their own in any program context. The music of Berio, Penderecki, or Stockhausen, while strong statements of advanced musical ideas of the twentieth century, should be left to major orchestras equipped to handle the notational and other intricacies of avant-garde music.

There are several sources of assistance available in discovering suitable contemporary music. The conductor should attend at least one of the annual conferences of the American Symphony Orchestra League where publishers display new works for examination. Publishers' representatives are knowledgeable, and happy to make suggestions to coincide with the resources of almost any orchestra.

The series of compositions commissioned and recorded by the Louisville Philharmonic Orchestra in Kentucky is another source. Every contemporary idiom is represented in the Louisville commission series, and the conductor may discover a composer new to him whose style is compatible with his orchestra. As Daniel Moe has suggested, "if you can't find any literature from this century that really excites you, seriously consider changing professions."[3]

The serious music departments of both ASCAP and BMI are treasuries of information about contemporary composers, their music, and the feasibility of these works for community orchestras. They are delighted and eager to share their information with any conductor seeking help in programming music of our time. The International Contemporary Music Exchange maintains a library and listening room in New York City.* Igor Buketoff, Director, is a conductor who has zealously promoted the exchange concept for over fifteen years.

Two additional sources for contemporary American music are the American Composers' Alliance and the American Music Center. The latter is the repository of all compositions commissioned by grants from the National Endowment for the Arts.

The conductor should first program contemporary music from a rather conservative stance, moving toward the more advanced styles of contemporary musical expression as the orchestra and audience become more receptive. It is far better for the conductor to advance steadily from a conservative position than to retreat hastily from a more advanced outpost.

OPERA AND ORATORIO PERFORMANCES

To achieve the widest possible variety in program content, opera and oratorio must be considered. Fully mounted or concert versions of opera in a season's concerts must be decided on the basis of facilities, available singers, and budget. Some guidelines are presented here which may be helpful.

*The Exchange is at 58 W. 58th Street, Suite 29B, New York, New York 10019.

If the orchestra is located in a metropolitan area where a resident opera company or college groups present opera each season, the community orchestra need not consider presenting opera. Such productions would then fulfill personal desires of orchestra and conductor, not community needs. In more remote communities, however, occasional operatic productions should be considered.

The choice of opera must take into consideration the availability of singers, rehearsal time, chorus, and money. Well-known works usually require a large chorus together with *compramario* (secondary) roles which are taken by local singers. Hiring all solo singers from "outside" requires too large an outlay from the orchestra budget. Operas which have little or no chorus, and few secondary roles, are often not so well known, and therefore have less box office appeal. Opera, even with a minimum of singers, sets, and costumes, is expensive and careful consideration must be given to financial as well as artistic matters.

Probably the most valuable source of information is the Central Opera Service.[4] It publishes a *Bulletin* several times each year, together with numerous special booklets and pamphlets containing information about repertoire, set and costume rental, sources of orchestra parts,* and other pertinent data.

Many opera orchestrations require rather sparse brass and woodwind writing (unless one is performing Wagner) so players have long rests before playing a few notes here and there. It can be boring for them, yet they must be alert for entrances which are far apart. For those players playing most of the time, the music is often less interesting than symphonic literature. It is no accident that one of the highest paid orchestras in the United States is the Metropolitan Opera Orchestra! Community orchestras exist as much for the players as for anyone and too much accompaniment in a given season will create morale problems.

Oratorio performances require less rehearsal time, are less expensive to produce than opera, and have a certain box office appeal. While some might argue the artistic merit of annual performances of Handel's *Messiah*, yet people do attend these who do not come to any other musical event. If an existing chorus is used for these performances, the initial choral preparation should be done by the regular chorus master, with the orchestra conductor directing the final piano rehearsals prior to putting chorus and orchestra together. In communities where no chorus exists, the orchestra conductor must recruit his own and train them. (A preliminary meeting with the ministerial association is most helpful in recruiting singers.)

---

*Contemporary operas are not covered by ASCAP or BMI blanket performing licenses. Royalties as well as rentals must be paid. Usually these fees can be negotiated with the publishers.

As a general rule in working with an existing chorus, the orchestra conductor conducts those performances that are on the orchestra's schedule of concerts. If the chorus borrows players for a concert, the chorus director will be the conductor. When such requests for players come to the orchestra, the conductor should encourage his players to help out: it is another aid in cementing community goodwill.

SCHOOL AND YOUTH CONCERTS

Concerts for school children are an integral part of the performance schedules of many orchestras.* These concerts are usually the first exposure to live serious music which children receive. Careful programming for these concerts is an absolute necessity. Planning concerts must be done in consultation with school music personnel, who are in a better position than the conductor to know the needs of the children.

If it is not feasible for the entire orchestra to present school programs, various chamber ensembles can be organized from within orchestra membership for this purpose. Smaller ensembles can be a better introduction to live music than the full orchestra, since the atmosphere is more relaxed. Programs should be highly varied, selections short, few slow and quiet works, and with a minimum of comment from the conductor. The best rule is to let the music speak for itself. Special lighting effects and other "gimmicks" should be avoided.

The most capable student musicians should be selected to appear on these programs. They may appear in short solo roles or as members of the orchestra, seated with adult musicians. School instrumental directors must be consulted about the use of student instrumentalists.

POP AND OTHER SPECIAL PROGRAMS

There is a demand for pop programs in most communities. This demand has undoubtedly been generated by the success of the Boston Pops Orchestra under Arthur Fiedler, the Mantovani Orchestra, and others.

For many persons, music in pop concerts should sound like Dr. Fiedler's music, but audiences are not aware that the arrangements he uses are his own and cannot be rented. They are conducted only by Dr. Fiedler. The same situation applies to arrangements by Mantovani, Bachrach, and other popular figures. Further, such arrangements are designed for highly skilled, professional musicians and are beyond the ability of many community orchestra musicians.

*Much valuable information can be obtained from a publication of the Bureau of Research, U.S. Department of Health, Education, and Welfare on the presentation of youth concerts. Complete information is listed in the Bibliography.

Popular concerts usually mean playing the music an audience knows. If the audience has no real familiarity with music, it is difficult to plan programs which will be entirely satisfactory. Typical pop programs include works which should be on the subscription programs of community orchestras. Including a Strauss waltz or a medley of Broadway show tunes on subscription programs may have a better effect than saving all these works for a once-a-year pop program.

Lighter music or popular classics deserve a place on community orchestra programs. The only question to be asked is, "Is this work a good piece regardless of its type?" *Quality*, not category, should be the governing priority. When a community orchestra achieves a stability in both its repertoire and audience, then it may be time to plan for special pop programs.

In communities where the orchestra's schedule is flexible there are special programs of service to the community which can and should be given. Some of the non-traditional avenues of service include small ensembles performing in schools and nursing homes where the full orchestra cannot go, or at special civic celebrations like dedications of new church facilities. Playing concerts on stages in a somber concert atmosphere is not the only function of a community orchestra.

When an orchestra makes the effort to move in wider spheres of activity beyond the concert arena, the orchestra's audience becomes more widespread, its financial base stronger, and the orchestra truly becomes a community endeavor. The more exposure an orchestra has, the more secure its future.

Certain kinds of memorial programs might be considered as well. During 1970, there were many programs celebrating the bicentenary of Beethoven's birth, and surely 1985 will prompt many concerts commemorating the three-hundredth anniversary of the birth of Johann Sebastian Bach. In tribute to the large Scandinavian population of Port Angeles, we performed an all-Scandinavian program featuring works of Grieg, Alfven, Gade, and Sibelius. Similar programs can be used to highlight the different ethnic and cultural backgrounds of nearly every community in the country.

SUMMARY

Specific program suggestions cannot be made for any orchestra without knowing its strengths and weaknesses. Program content will most likely fit the musical taste of a community in following such guidelines as variety, including solo vehicles, presentation of choral and/or operatic works, pop concerts, and special programs for the entire orchestra or smaller ensembles. The most important first step is the determination of the actual tastes and desires of the community.

chapter 7

Specific Program Suggestions

Program content for any orchestra is a highly individual matter, reflecting the tastes of the community and the background of training and personal preferences of the conductor.* The conductor must bear in mind that while he must present a variety of material on his programs, he should not keep portions of his orchestra (e.g., the brass section) idle for too much of the time.

The Romantic orchestral literature contains most of the "hit parade" of the total orchestral repertoire. Many of these works are beyond the abilities of smaller community orchestras, even though they are the very things most audiences want to hear. In one sense, the community orchestra must then "compete" with recorded versions by the world's greatest orchestras and conductors: an unfair disadvantage, at best.

Although many community orchestras have fine members in all sections, they lack the depth in the strings to create the lush sound of the major recording orchestras. It is the thin string sound in particular that weakens performances of Tchaikovsky, Brahms, Bruckner and Wagner. Program content must be carefully planned to determine which works of these and similar composers can be performed well, without the orchestra suffering unfair comparisons with recordings. Three distinct things go into the balanced planning of symphony programs: "(1) a judicious use of the relatively few numbers which are both 'classics' and genuinely enjoyed; (2) the employment, more sparingly, of numbers less popular than

---

*The repertoire of many conductors is a direct outgrowth of their training in conducting classes or their experience as orchestral players. Thus it is often limited to the standard fare of the mainstream of music.

they once were but having an inherent musical value; and (3) the addition to the repertoire of new works of real significance."[1]

There are many works which "sound" like the better known ones which can—and in some situations *must*—be substituted for the "ten all-time symphonic hits." The search for suitable substitutions must be made diligently and is never-ending. Conductors must be aware, however, of the wisdom of John Sherman's comment, "There never was (never will be) unanimity of satisfaction with symphony program content."[2]

SYMPHONIES

Of major symphonic works of the Classical period, the symphonies of Haydn and Mozart can be considered "fair game." While certain problems are present in the string parts, most community orchestras can meet the challenge. It would be better to avoid the last three Mozart symphonies, and No. 34 in C (K. 388) has the problem of divided violas for the entire slow movement. A little searching might uncover an occasional Mannheim School "gem." Obviously, certain of the Mozart-Haydn group must be avoided, and care must be taken to preserve the inherent delicacy and grace of whichever of these composers' works are selected.

Beethoven and Schubert symphonies are highly popular, well-known, and no orchestra's programs are complete without their inclusion. Of the Beethoven works, certainly the First, Second and Eighth can be performed; with some depth in the strings and adequate rehearsal time, the Fifth can be done as well.* The Third and Seventh have more problems, while the Sixth is perhaps the most difficult; the Ninth, of course, has its own special problems of solo voices, chorus, and plainly difficult orchestra writing throughout.

Schubert's "Great" in C major (variously known as No. 7, No. 9, or No. 10) should not appear on most community orchestra programs because it is difficult for both orchestra and audience. The Second, Fifth and Sixth ought to be played more often than they are; also the Fourth ("Tragic") is, unfortunately, rarely heard. These four, together with the Eighth ("Unfinished") can well represent Schubert for several seasons.

Mendelssohn stands at the crossroads between the Classical and Romantic periods. Although the Fourth ("Italian") is his most popular symphony, it is also the most difficult. The Third ("Scotch") is not played nearly as often, but is very appealing and well within the capabilities of most orchestras. The Fifth ("Reformation") has some string problems in the first and fourth movements but should be considered, especially since it does utilize trombones.

The four Schumann symphonies begin to present some of the prob-

---

*With the added advantage of utilizing trombones.

lems that recur later in Tchaikovsky and Brahms. For example, each has thick string writing necessary to support the deeper brass. Schumann's somewhat awkward orchestration requires much attention to balance and his writing for upper strings is highly pianistic. The Fourth Symphony is perhaps the most likely community-orchestra candidate. If the orchestra has a very good horn section, the Third ("Rhenish") would be a possibility. The First ("Spring") has some very difficult violin parts and is perhaps best left to more professional orchestras. The Second may be too long for some orchestras and too unknown for some audience.

Of the four Brahms works in the genre, only the Second qualifies as community-orchestra material, and even this work has difficulties enough, particularly in the second movement. The First is very difficult with its cross rhythms and thick string texture. Unless the orchestra has four excellent horn players, together with good, accurate trombones, the chorale in the final movement will not sound well. The introspective character of the Third may pose difficulties for the audience as well as the orchestra. Most community orchestra string sections are not deep enough to sustain the sound demanded by the Fourth.

As suitable substitutions, one should give consideration to the Serenades, especially the first in D Major. The Second Serenade does not utilize all of the strings, but could be considered on a special program that uses various sections of the orchestra. The Variations on a Theme of Haydn also can, with plenty of diligent rehearsing, appear on most community orchestra programs.

Because of the enormous melodic appeal of the music of Tchaikovsky, his major works have been played and recorded many times. The last three symphonies constitute his major efforts in symphonic form, but because of the great difficulties present in each of these scores, most community orchestras ought to avoid them; however, the first three symphonies must be considered. (If the orchestra boasts an excellent solo hornist, the Fifth Symphony is a possibility.) They do not have the difficulties in the string parts, nor do they require the intensity of string support for the brass, yet Tchaikovsky sound and style are present.

Although Antonín Dvořák composed nine symphonies, only the "New World" enjoys the popularity which some of the others deserve. The symphony is difficult, and if there is not an English Horn player or instrument available, the slow movement loses its flavor. The G Major Symphony (No. 8, Op. 88) is an ideal Romantic symphony for any community orchestra because most of the more important material is given to those instruments which are strongest in community orchestras. The D Major (No. 6, Op. 60) is almost totally unknown. Both symphonies are exempt from the difficulties of his other symphonic works, are full of gracious melodic material, and are enjoyable for both orchestra and audience. The first five symphonies have much to commend them, but contain some complexities in the inner string parts which might be too formidable for some community orchestras.

The symphonies which bridge the gap between the Romantic and contemporary periods (Bruckner, Mahler, Rachmaninov, Sibelius, Nielsen) must be examined, but most of them are generally too difficult and too long for the "average" community orchestra. Certainly Bruckner, Mahler, and Rachmaninov fall within that category. The Third by Nielsen and the Second and Fifth of Sibelius could be programmed with a moderate depth in the string section.

A few composers of the twentieth century wrote in symphonic form, particularly the Soviet composers, and Ralph Vaughan Williams in England. For the most part, these works should be left to the major orchestras, including the "Classical" Symphony by Prokofiev. They are very difficult for all sections of the orchestra, requiring rehearsal time out of proportion to the balance of the program. However, the Fifth Symphony by Vaughan Williams could be a candidate for performance.

There are even fewer symphonies by contemporary American composers. Of the few available, the Second Symphony by Howard Hanson, the Third by Robert Ward, and the Third of Roy Harris are within the capabilities of some of our community orchestras. In addition, some attention might be given to works in symphonic form by both Peter Mennin and the late Walter Piston.

Certain symphonic works, particularly of the Romantic era, have fallen from the favor they once had. For example, the First Symphony of Vassili Kalinnikov is melodically as attractive as Tchaikovsky, and far less difficult. The "Antar" Symphony of Rimsky-Korsakov is rarely heard. Borodin's Second does receive performances from time to time. One other composer who should return to the repertoire is Joachim Raff. His "Im Walde" Symphony, although rather Brucknerian in character, is not too difficult and could be played by most orchestras.

The Symphony in D Minor of Franck has somewhat the same problems of the Dvořák "New World" in that the English horn solo must be there. Conductors might consider substituting the Chausson Symphony in B flat, or one of the Gounod symphonies when considering French music.

Conductors might also look at the symphonies of the Swedish composer Franz Berwald as another possibility.

OVERTURES

For concert openers, almost any Mozart overture can be played by most community orchestras including the Overture to *The Marriage of Figaro*. This overture requires a particularly agile string section, especially if the conductor prefers a very fast *Presto*. However, the tempo indication must be thought of in terms of the common-time signature, not *alla breve*; thus the *Presto* is not really so fast, and can be performed.

Beethoven overtures are useful, particularly if the conductor looks beyond *Leonore No. 3*. Certainly *Egmont* and *Coriolan* can be played by almost any orchestra. If the violins cannot negotiate the intricacies of the *Leonore*, *Fidelio* could be substituted. *Namensfeier* and *King Stephen* are hardly ever played, while *Consecration of the House* is a sort of special-occasion piece.

Rossini overtures should be played more often than they are. Certain ones pose special problems for various sections,* but many can easily be used either at the beginning or end of a concert. The overtures of Auber fall into the same category. They tend toward lightness and have much audience appeal. There was a time when von Suppe and Herold were "regulars" on concert programs, but their music has fallen from favor. It may be time to return both to the concert hall.

There are other Mendelssohn overtures beside *Fingal's Cave*. Of the several, *Calm Sea and Prosperous Voyage, The Fair Melusine*, and *Ruy Blas* receive far more performances in England than in America. They should be revived here, as they are good examples of Mendelssohn's style and are not too difficult for any section of the orchestra.

Overtures from the latter part of the nineteenth century pose some of the same difficulties as symphonies: thick string textures and highly involved string passages create rehearsal problems out of proportion to their length.

In this category, the two overtures of Brahms certainly fit. Others of like nature are those by Wagner, although the Preludes to *Die Meistersinger* and *Tannhauser* can be played by some orchestras. There is a difference between concert overtures by Brahms and Dvořák and the opera overtures of the latter part of the century. Verdi overtures—for example, *Sicilian Vespers* and *La Forza del Destino*—can be played by most community orchestras.

There are many good curtain raisers written by American composers of the twentieth century: works to fit almost any orchestral combination and condition. Publishers are most happy to call these works to the attention of conductors, and both ASCAP and BMI offices can offer helpful suggestions.

TONE POEMS AND SUITES

Many concert programs need a work longer than an overture, or a work which could substitute for a symphony. There are many orchestral

---

*La Scala di Seta, for example, contains some of the most treacherous oboe and bassoon writing in the entire orchestra literature.

works, particularly of the Romantic period, which fill this requirement.

When one thinks of tone poems, Richard Strauss and Liszt immediately come to mind. Unfortunately, most community orchestras do not have the players in all sections capable of giving adequate performances of these works. There are other composers whose music is somewhat easier, yet of very high quality, which can sound excellent played by orchestras of limited ability.

Bedřich Smetana immediately brings to mind *The Moldau*. However, there are five other works in the *My Fatherland* cycle, of which *Tabor* and *From Bohemia's Fields and Forests* deserve special consideration. The latter has a passage for strings which is rather difficult, but it can be worked out with a little extra effort.

Dvořák's tone poems are perhaps too obscure for most audiences, although they contain some lovely music. *The Wood Dove*, Op. 107, is particularly effective; it contains a very beautiful trumpet solo, and most community orchestras have at least one trumpet player capable of playing a long, *cantabile* line. Although the *Scherzo Capriccioso*, Op. 66, is difficult in places (due in part to the awkward key signature of five flats), it should be considered as well as the "In Nature's Realm" overture, Op. 91.

Ballet suites seem to have been either relegated to the pop concert programs or neglected entirely. The Romantic period witnessed the flowering of classical ballet: suites from such ballets as *Coppelia*, *Sylvia*, *Swan Lake*, and *Sleeping Beauty*, to name but four, have much audience appeal and should be performed. *The Nutcracker* is perhaps too well-known and is rather difficult; unless the orchestra is quite well endowed with good strings and solo winds, it might be well to avoid it.

Many of the operas of the nineteenth century have long ballet sequences. Surely, no audience can be bored with the ballet scenes from *Faust* or *Aida*. The music is appealing and not difficult. The ballet music from Massenet's *Le Cid*, once very popular, should also be considered.

Of earlier ballet music, the complete *Prometheus* music of Beethoven is rarely performed as is the incidental music to *The Ruins of Athens*. The complete *Egmont* music, again by Beethoven, requires chorus and solo voices which might make it less feasible. Incidental music to stage works by Bizet (*L'Arlésienne*), Grieg (*Peer Gynt* and *Sigurd Jorsalfar*) or Fauré (Pelleas) and many others ought also to be considered.

Serenades of Mozart and Haydn contain much delightful music which is not generally performed. They are perhaps not quite so difficult as Mozart symphonies, and have much of the same flavor. The orchestral suites of Bach also can be considered.

Sibelius was especially fond of the tone poem. However, these works have much *divisi* string writing which precludes their inclusion on the programs of many community orchestras. Although the notes themselves are not so difficult, dividing into three and four parts creates a thinness of texture which Sibelius did not intend.

There are many ballet and other suites from the contemporary period which can be performed by community orchestras. Stravinsky's ballet suites, particularly *Firebird*, *Petrouchka*, and *The Rites of Spring*, are well known but with the possible exception of *Firebird* are generally too difficult for community orchestras. The Suite from *Pulchinella* and the two early suites for orchestra have far better chances of good performances and should be considered when looking for more contemporary works.

The Soviet composers have written much music which falls within the capabilities of community orchestras. There are, of course, the rental and royalty fees which might price these works out of community-orchestra budgets. Much playable music of the ballet genre has been written by American composers as well. Conductors would do well to consult with publishers as to what is available. The tendency to program well-known works (*Appalachian Spring* by Copland is a good example) should be avoided, although the Four Dance Episodes from *Rodeo* are well within the capabilities of most orchestras. Many were written for the major orchestras and their difficulties are more than most community orchestras can handle well. A ballet score which has much the same flavor of the Copland, yet is much easier to perform well is Hunter Johnson's *Letter to the World*, written for Martha Graham's dance company.

WORKS FOR SOLO INSTRUMENT(S)

In addition to the usual concerto literature which visiting soloists would normally choose, there is a large number of works which a conductor can program, using soloists from the orchestra.

Most community orchestra first-chair wind players could perform the Mozart *Sinfonia Concertante for Winds*, K. Anh. 9. If the concertmaster is quite good, Bach's *Brandenburg* Concerto No. 4 is another work which can be performed well by most community orchestras, as the flute parts are not too difficult.

Vehicles using solo winds, especially flute and clarinet, are plentiful from both Classical and Romantic periods and from the twentieth century. For example, flute concertos by Mozart, the suite for flute by Telemann, clarinet concertos by Weber and Mozart, the shorter works for flute by Griffes and Kennan, and the Suite for Clarinet by Ernst Krenek. These are some of the works which community orchestras ought to use featuring soloists from the orchestra.

Many community orchestras also have excellent brass players. Trumpet concertos are a novelty. As a change from the endless parade of pianists and violinists, a program featuring the orchestra's solo trumpet in the Hummel concerto, for example, would be welcome. If the orchestra has two good trumpet players, concertos for two trumpets by Vivaldi and Manfredini are generally available.

French horn players grow up on the four concertos by Mozart. In addition, there is his Concert Rondo, as well as concertos by other composers. If the orchestra has a good horn section (not too uncommon in our time), Schumann's Concertpiece for Four Horns, Op. 86, is a very attractive candidate. The conductor who seeks out solo players from among his own personnel will also help build orchestra morale: *all good soloists are not necessarily imported.*

USE OF SMALLER ENSEMBLES

The use of smaller ensembles can bring more variety to the program, as well as providing the audience with exposure to literature which they might not otherwise have an opportunity to hear. If, on any given program, most of the works use heavy brass sparingly, then thought could be given to including a special number featuring brass choir; or there might be a wind quintet or string quartet rehearsing on their own. Such groups ought to be used wherever possible.

There is a huge repertoire of works using only the string section, from the Baroque to the present day. The use of the strings alone can be an effective device of program contrast. There are many pieces of varying difficulty which can be performed by community orchestra string sections.

The conductor must encourage players to develop ensembles on their own time, if possible. This can be an effective contrast not only on the regular concerts, but an ideal means of introducing school children to the various sounds of the orchestra. And the conductor should be available to help these smaller groups, when invited.

CHORAL WORKS

Although many communities do not boast a large and versatile choral group, most of them find enough singers to present annual performances of *Messiah.* The number of such performances each year might lead one to suspect that this is the only Christmas work that uses soloists, chorus, and orchestra. (It may be that this is the only work a community can recognize!) The *Christmas Oratorio* of Saint-Saens is a delightful substitute for endless *Messiah* performances. If the choral group is large enough, *The Childhood of Christ* by Berlioz can be done effectively, although it is more difficult for both orchestra and chorus. It requires a good harpist. The harp part in the Saint-Saens can be realized on the piano without too much loss of effect, but the harp is absolutely necessary for the Berlioz unless the conductor omits the serenade for two flutes and harp in the third part of the trilogy.

Most community choruses are not up to the Bach *Christmas Oratorio*, nor do many orchestras have the trumpet players skilled in high, *clarino* writing. The parts can be played on C clarinets, but must be doubled to get an effect closer to trumpets. *A Child of Our Time* by the British composer Michael Tippett is too difficult for community orchestras and choruses. If the right singers are available, a staged, tableau, or concert performance of Menotti's *Amahl and the Night Visitors* is a possible alternative for the annual *Messiah.* Conductors will feel pressure to perform the Handel annually, but should insist, at least once in a while, on a change of Christmas musical fare. Diligent searching through publisher's catalogues will turn up other possibilities.

There are many other occasions besides Christmas for the use of chorus on orchestral programs. In addition to the major oratorio literature, there are smaller choral-orchestral works such as the part-songs of Brahms, the *Choral Fantasy* by Beethoven (if a good pianist is available), Schubert and Mozart masses, or even a program of well-known opera choruses. Such variety can stimulate audience growth, for when a chorus appears at a regular subscription concert all their friends and relatives will turn out, even though they are not regular subscribers.

MISCELLANEOUS WORKS

Very often the inclusion of an encore-type piece on a program will provide a necessary contrast which might otherwise be missing. Such pieces as an occasional Strauss waltz, a Slavonic Dance of Dvořák, or one of LeRoy Anderson's works will do wonders for audience enthusiasm. These pieces do not demean a concert; if they help build enthusiasm for the orchestra, they will strengthen the entire orchestra program.

SUMMARY

Programming is a highly individual effort; much program content depends on both conductor and orchestra. For many community orchestras, judicious substitution for the "ten greatest symphonic hits" with works which "sound" like them will serve the orchestra well and keep the audience happy.

Programming works utilizing orchestra members as soloists, featuring community choral groups whenever possible, and putting shorter, pop-type works on the subscription concerts from time to time will help increase audience enthusiasm for the orchestra as well as for the more substantial symphonic fare.

chapter 8

Actual Program Practice

In an effort to elicit opinions and comments concerning overall programming policies, questionnaires were circulated to a number of community orchestras and conductors throughout the country. Each orchestra was also invited to submit programs for seasons 1970 through 1973. Our survey was limited specifically to community orchestras, whereas the other surveys mentioned either covered major orchestras only (Mueller), or else a much larger combination of all types and sizes of orchestras and seasons (BMI).*

The response was not as representative of community orchestras as could be desired, but certain conclusions can be drawn. The light response may be attributed to two factors: the questionnaire was circulated in late April 1973, a time when most community orchestras are concluding their seasons, and since many community orchestras do not maintain office staffs, conductors must do most of this clerical work themselves.

Most orchestras play a variety of concerts—subscription, pop, youth, and other special programs. Limiting the program survey to subscription concerts proved inadvisable, since many of the other types of programs are included in subscription series and what may be a "serious" effort by one orchestra is a pop or youth concert for another.

At gatherings of conductors, one hears talk about the pressures placed on them concerning program material. Thus, the first question on the questionnaire was, "As a conductor, do you feel minimal, occasional, or frequent pressure concerning program content?" The conductors re-

*Although the program survey was conducted for the seasons 1970-73, perusal of many orchestra programs since that time indicate little change in programming trends.

sponded:* no pressure — 1; minimal pressure — 12; occasional pressure — 9; frequent pressure — 2.

The source of pressure on the responding conductors seemed to be rather evenly spread among the several sources: board members — 10; subscribers — 8; orchestra members — 9; all of the above — 3;** music critic — 1; women's association — 1.

The conductors were asked to explain briefly how they managed to keep themselves and others satisfied as to program content. The answers overwhelmingly stressed "balance." Some conductors elaborated with additional comments:

> I program primarily to please myself. However, my musical taste is eclectic and my programs rather commercial.
>
> By balancing the programs, and giving a certain number of pot-boilers, I keep the carpers happy, and thereby have a certain amount of freedom regarding the rest of the program.***
>
> After all, the board, guild, etc., did not go to music school and does not know the repertoire. The conductor gets paid, in part, for making the best choices.
>
> Try for balance that provides musical challenge and growth for conductor and orchestra with audience appeal as well. Not always easy to do and also difficult to explain. . . .
>
> I program music I believe in; I avoid any music which is too difficult to learn well in our limited rehearsal schedule; I avoid overdone "war houses"; I select certain contemporary works which will attract rather than repel our audiences, in an effort to develop a sympathetic and receptive attitude toward contemporary music.
>
> Where the suggestions are along lines of my own convictions, I endeavor to include them, balancing such with total programming.

For the most part, the programs submitted with the questionnaires seem to follow the ideals set forth by the conductors. It must be remem-

---

*The author's personal experience in fifteen years conducting the Port Angeles Symphony was "frequent" early in his tenure, declining to "minimal" in the last few seasons. The programs did not change materially, rather, the audience and orchestra came to accept the programming philosophy.

**Again, the author's personal experience tends to bear this out, although in his case, subscribers were somewhat reluctant to comment directly to him. How many board comments actually came secondhand from subscribers is impossible to ascertain.

***In a covering letter this conductor added, "On our 'serious' concerts, there is at least one pot-boiler, to get the audience into the hall, but as I said on the questionnaire, I do not feel that a community orchestra should devote the bulk of its programming to works that the audience is used to hearing on the radio or played in concert by professionals."

bered that most of the conductors submitting programs have had several years of experience; it might be interesting to investigate and compare programs for their first three seasons against their choices as they matured.

Finally, the survey presented a list of ten compositions.* The conductors were asked to indicate which ones "perhaps the average community orchestra should not perform." Once more, there was a high degree of unanimity regarding suitability for inclusion in the "average" community orchestra program. Table I lists these ten works with the number of "no" votes as to their suitability for community orchestra programming, together with the number of performances the ten actually received on programs submitted.

If the figures in Table I are compared with those compiled by Broadcast Music, Inc.[1] for the 1969-70 concert season (the season prior to the ones collated on the present survey), all sizes of orchestras show some correlation with the figures in our survey, relative to nineteenth-century composition; the greatest deviation is with major and metropolitan orchestras which are better equipped to deal with the complexities of more contemporary compositions.

TABLE I

		Number of No Votes	Actual Performances
Beethoven	Symphony III	2	3
Berlioz	Symphony Fantastique	17	0
Brahms	Symphony I	3	4
Tchaikovsky	Symphony VI	3	2
Dvořák	Symphony IX	2	1
Debussy	La Mer	20	0
Stravinsky	Petrouchka	17	0
Bartok	Concerto for Orchestra	21	0
Copland	Appalachian Spring	4	1
Prokofiev	"Classical" Symphony	12	1

*The compositions were selected from the programs of a community orchestra known to the present writer and which did not take part in the survey. At the time the programs were announced, questions were raised as to the advisability of programming these works, with that orchestra.

Table II shows the total of all performances by 626 orchestras partici-
pating in the BMI survey, together with the number of different recorded
versions of the same works found in the Schwann Catalogue of Records
and Tapes. The difference in number of recorded performances of the
Berlioz in Table II compared to the number of "no" votes for that work
in Table I may be attributed, in part, to the fact that the composition is
a very good hi-fi or stereo demonstration piece and it is also a good orchestra display work. The major orchestras are the orchestras which play
the most concerts, both subscription and tour, and make recordings. It
is a practice to perform works on tour which the orchestra has recorded,
to stimulate record sales.

The capabilities of community orchestras vary widely, and conductors
should usually program within the framework of what is feasible, given
the limited rehearsal time and orchestra ability. However, it appears that
programs include the better known, if not easier, works of any composer.
Since works become better known through repeated performances and a
larger number of recorded versions, programming these works shows an
inclination on the part of the conductor to play it safe. Likewise, requests
from audience and board members will be for those works which are
usually most familiar.

Two hundred twenty-four programs from nineteen community orchestras submitting programs were analyzed (see Appendix D). Table III
shows the number of composers, individual compositions, and total
number of performances, by historical period, with percentages of the
total for each category.

TABLE II

		Number of Performances by Orchestras in BMI Survey	*Number of Recorded Versions*
Bethoven	Symphony III	115	28
Berlioz	Symphony Fantastique	78	24
Brahms	Symphony I	88	22
Tchaikovsky	Symphony VI	79	26
Dvořák	Symphony IX	127	23
Debussy	La Mer	52	18
Stravinsky	Petrouchka	49	8
Bartok	Concerto for Orchestra	59	11
Copland	Appalachian Spring	13	12
Prokofiev	"Classical" Symphony	162	17

TABLE III

	Number of Composers	%	Number of Works*	%	Number of Perform-ances	%
Baroque and Pre-Baroque	9	(3.8)	36	(5.7)	48	(5.5)
Classical	13**	(5.6)	96	(15.3)	147	(16.9)
Romantic	55	(23.4)	205	(32.7)	301	(34.6)
Contemporary, non-US***	55	(23.4)	124	(19.7)	168	(19.3)
Contemporary, US	101	(43.3)	166	(26.4)	205	(23.5)
Total****	233	(99.5)	627	(99.8)	869	(99.8)

*For the sake of convenience, performances of sections of longer works (arias, etc.) were considered as individual compositions.

**All of Beethoven and Schubert are totaled within the Classical period, even though many of the compositions are quite Romantic in flavor.

***Contemporary, non-United States composers include numbers of immigrants who came to this country immediately before and after World War II. The determining criterion was where the largest share of their training occurred, e.g., Menotti is considered a United States composer because he studied here although he was born in Italy, while Ernst Bloch is non-United States because he came after he had become a mature composer.

****Percentage figures were rounded to the first number after the decimal point.

The number of contemporary United States composers appears very high in comparison with other periods and would seem to indicate a large, vital interest in the music of these composers. Subtracting the number of composers and compositions which are markedly lighter or pop in character, the picture is altered significantly, as shown in Table IV.

Philip Hart pointed up this exhaustive survey of American symphony orchestras as follows:

Some evidence in the BMI surveys indicates a higher percentage of American music in the nonsubscription—popular, children's and summer—concerts than in the subscription programs; for the one year (1968-69) in which a breakdown of data is reported, subscription and tour concerts contained 15.4% of American music, while the others had 24.2%. This can be explained by the fact that in both of the last two years reported there was a substantially higher proportion (4.82%) of popular and show music on the nonsubscription programs than on subscription and tour concerts (1.12%) between 1968 and 1970.[2]

TABLE IV

Comparison of "Serious" and "Pop" Programming
for Contemporary U.S. Composers

	Number of Composers	%	Number of Works	%	Number of Perform-ances	%
"Pop"	38	(37.6)	66	(39.7)	90	(43.9)
"Serious"	63	(62.3)	100	(60.4)	115	(56.1)
Total	101	(99.9)	166	(101.1)	205	(100.0)

Table V inserts this dividing line of "serious" vs. "pop" music into Table III, showing that while the "serious" contemporary American composer is receiving performances, the percentage of performances is indeed small. Over half of the works and performances are those of before the twentieth century thus validating the claim that programs are too much devoted to "ancestor worship."[3]

Figures are not available on the length of playing time, and these probably reduce the total number of minutes of exposure to contemporary serious music by American composers even more. Although the total number of American composers represented is high, the number of works performed (100) and the total number of performances (115) of serious contemporary music seems disappointing. That is, single performances are frequent enough, but very few works get played more than once in the season. Many conductors will do "first performances" but will not program works already premiered by other conductors. The few works which did receive additional performances were naturally the ones more or less established in the repertoire. While the sampling is small, we suspect it to be indicative of a widespread practice.*

The small number of Baroque composers can be explained by the fact that little of this music utilizes the entire orchestra. Conductors of community orchestras tend to program works which use all of the orchestra most of the time, accepting the proposition that community orchestras exist more for the players than for anyone else. This is also evidenced by more performances of later Haydn and Mozart than of earlier works.

Baroque composers most represented were, as might be expected, Bach, Handel, Vivaldi, and Corelli. Telemann, Gabrielli, Locatelli and Pidilla were also performed, but less often.

*The figures given by Philip Hart (cited in note 2) give some credence to this suspicion.

TABLE V

	Number of Composers	%	Number of Works	%	Number of Perform- ances	%
Baroque	9	(3.8)	36	(5.7)	48	(5.5)
Classical	13	(5.6)	96	(15.3)	147	(16.9)
Romantic	55	(23.4)	205	(32.7)	301	(34.6)
Contemporary— non-US	55	(23.4)	124	(19.7)	168	(19.3)
Contemporary— US "Serious"	63	(27.0)	100	(15.9)	115	(13.2)
Contemporary— US "Pop"	38	(16.3)	66	(10.5)	90	(10.4)

Of Classical period composers, Mozart was the most often performed (52 performances), followed by Beethoven (40), Haydn (17), Schubert (15) and Rossini (11). Johann Christian Bach, Boccherini, Gluck and Pergolesi each received two performances; C.P.E. Bach, Cherubini, Dragonetti, and Antonio Rolla were limited to one performance each. Perhaps had Dragonetti not written his *Concerto for Double Bass*, one one would never hear of him at all. No Mannheim school compositions were performed.

The most frequently played work by Mozart was the Overture to *The Marriage of Figaro* (5), followed by the Symphony No. 40 (4), and the Piano Concerto in D minor, No. 20, and *Requiem Mass*, each with three performances. The balance of Mozart performances was fairly evenly spread over works of all genres. It is interesting that the symphonies which most community orchestras can play particularly well, No. 35 in D ("Haffner"), No. 36 in C ("Linz"), and No. 38 in D ("Prague") were not performed at all. Nos. 40 and 41 are probably the most difficult, yet they received most of the performances—another tribute to playing what is best known.

All of Beethoven's symphonies were performed, but the most popular were No. 5 and No. 7 (4 performances each), No. 3 (3), and Nos. 4, 6 and 8 with two performances each. All of the concertos, except the Second Piano Concerto, were heard, as well as most of the overtures. The *Egmont* overture ranked with the Fifth and Seventh symphonies with four performances.

Although Haydn wrote much music for orchestra, only twelve of his compositions were heard on these programs. Of over one hundred symphonies, only five were played, and three (Nos. 45, 101, and 104) each had two performances. His most popular work was the Trumpet Concerto.

Schubert's Eighth ("Unfinished") remains a staple of the repertoire with five performances. Both the Fifth and Ninth ("The Great") each received two hearings, and the others no performances at all. It would appear that many conductors are depriving their audiences of some of Schubert's most delightful music—the Second, Fourth and Sixth Symphonies.

Rossini overtures are popular, judging from the programs examined. However, the once-loved *William Tell* overture was not played. It may be that overexposure in a nonconcert context diminishes the appeal of a work. One might wonder if the same fate will befall the beautiful slow movement of Mozart's Piano Concerto No. 21 in C since it graced television commercials for dog food and coffee in the 1970s.

The music of the Romantic era forms the largest portion of the community orchestra repertoire. That was the period of the flowering of the orchestra as we know it, together with a compositional style which stressed highly accessible melodic writing coupled with rich harmonic textures: music almost custom tailored for large audiences. The virtuoso conductor was born during the period, and the music written for orchestra nurtured his growth.

The ten most performed composers were Tchaikovsky, Verdi, and Brahms (each with 22 performances), Mendelssohn (21), Wagner (20), Dvořák (15), Johann Strauss, Jr. (14), Berlioz (13), Saint-Saens (12), and Rimsky-Korsakov (11). Following the "top ten," Bizet, Grieg and Schumann were tied with nine performances each, and Max Bruch was next with seven. However, Bruch would have barely counted at all had it not been for six performances of his G minor Violin Concerto, together with Berlioz' "Rakoczy" March, the works most often played of the period.

Tchaikovsky's last three symphonies were all performed, the Fourth and Sixth twice, but the earlier ones were not played. The Bb minor Piano Concerto and the Violin Concerto received performances, but not the "Rococo" Variations for Cello. *Swan Lake*, *Nutcracker*, and *Sleeping Beauty*, or portions of them, were also heard.

Brahms' First Symphony and *Requiem* each received four performances, the Fourth Symphony three, and *Academic Festival Overture*, Piano Concerto No. 2, and the Haydn Variations each received two performances. The two middle symphonies were not performed at all, which seems unusual since the Second is generally considered the symphony most nearly within the reach of most community orchestras.

Verdi performances may be attributed to a renewed interest in opera in the United States. Brahms and Tchaikovsky both far outweigh Verdi in performance time, since most of the Verdi pieces were individual arias. Wagner, on the other hand, received performances of the longer orchestral excerpts and overtures. The increasing number of performances of Wagner operas in the 1970s by opera companies, coupled with the large number of operatic works performed in the programs examined here, does attest to a new enthusiasm for opera in general.

Performances of Mendelssohn's music, again, reflected the trend to program that which is familiar. Both the Violin Concerto and the complete *Midsummernight's Dream** music received four performances, while the "Italian" Symphony and the First Piano Concerto had three. The Third ("Scotch") Symphony, another work within the capability of almost any orchestra, was not performed.

Dvořák's music seems to have countered the trend toward the "tried and true," with only one performance of the "New World," balanced by one performance of the *Sixth Symphony in D*, so reminiscent of the Brahms' *Second*. The Slavonic Dances continue to be as popular as they were when first published.

Johann Strauss is perhaps the most truly popular composer of the Romantic period. His music usually appears in programs of a lighter character, and is often used to close a program of more mixed fare. *Tales from the Vienna Woods* was the most performed, but the once-popular *Blue Danube* was heard only once.

Berlioz' appearance in the "top ten" is perhaps surprising. His music is very colorful, but generally very difficult for community orchestras. The *Roman Carnival* is a good orchestral display piece and perhaps one of the easier of his works. The "Rakoczy" March from *The Damnation of Faust*, with six performances, was the most performed and was responsible for thrusting Berlioz into the top group.

Saint-Saens in another composer one might not expect to find near the top of the list; three performances each of the Violin Concerto No. 3 and the *Carnival of the Animals* made it possible. One might have expected performances of the Second and Fourth piano concertos, but neither was heard; the once-popular *Danse Macabre* also was not performed.

Four performances each of *Capriccio Espagnol* and the *Russian Easter Overture* contributed to Rimsky-Korsakov's eleven performances, but *Scheherazade* was not performed. The work is very difficult, and very well known, and it may be that conductors chose to avoid the work for those reasons.

It is somewhat surprising that Robert Schumann's music was performed as infrequently as it was. The Piano Concerto in A minor received four performances, but only the First and Fourth symphonies were played.

Besides those already named, the remaining composers were represented only once, or one or two compositions received two performances. Works

*The programs did not distinguish between the complete *Midsummernight's Dream* score and the suite drawn from it.

which might be considered "pops" in character, other than Strauss waltzes, were heard ("Berceuse" from *Jocelyn* by Godard, and "Musical Snuff Box" by Liadov, to name but two), however, not in great numbers. Herold's *Zampa* overture was performed three times, and three von Suppe overtures were performed once each, but not the overtures of Auber.

Community orchestra programs avoided Mahler, Bruckner, and Reger almost completely. Mahler received four performances of three works, while Bruckner and Reger were limited to one performance each. Mahler's song-cycles can be performed by smaller orchestras, but the longer symphonic works are best left to more professional groups.

Performances of music by composers of the twentieth century who were not American-trained followed the basic trend of previous eras; conductors programmed works which were either well known, or seem to be logical musical outgrowths of earlier music. Composers with the most performances included Stravinsky (13), Vaughan Williams (13), Debussy (9), Prokofiev (8), Sibelius (8), Puccini (7), and Felix Labunski and Joaquin Rodrigo with five.

The eight performances of all or part of the *Firebird* ballet music contributed greatly to Stravinsky's popularity. Again, this work is well known and is perhaps the easiest to perform of his major compositions. Vaughan Williams was perhaps a surprising name, but his music is accessible to almost any orchestra and audience, and while there are difficult places in many of the pieces, the performance problems are not without solution.

Some of the composers, e.g., Sibelius, Rachmaninov, and Puccini, could perhaps have been included with the Romantic period, but they produced most of their music in the present century, hence their inclusion with this group.

Soviet composers' music usually has some compelling melodic interest and thus would be favored. Prokofiev's *Lt. Kije* and *Peter and the Wolf* accounted for over half of his performances. Three performances of Shostakovich's Fifth Symphony raised his total. Other Soviet composers were not so well represented because their music is not so well-known in the United States, with perhaps the exception of Khachaturian and Kabalevsky ballets.

In both the non-American and American composer categories of twentieth-century misic, the trend seems to be to sample one or two works of a composer rather than to present a broader spectrum of his music. Some of this may be due to the huge quantity of music being written in the present century; conductors do not have enough time to become acquainted with all of one composer's works, not to mention many composers' works. Conductors have been raised with music of past eras, and while a conductor might not have conducted the Tchaikovsky Fifth Symphony, for example, at least he is on familiar ground having heard Tchaikovsky for years. Coming to a totally new score is an entirely different matter.

American composers fared quite well, as may be seen from Table III. Of the 101 composers receiving performances, LeRoy Anderson led the list with twenty, followed by Aaron Copland with fifteen. These were the only composers receiving over ten performances. Charles Ives ranked third with eight, including three performances of William Schuman's arrangement of "Variations on America." After Ives came Howard Hanson (6), Gershwin, Hovhaness, Rodgers and Romberg (5 each), and Morton Gould, Victor Herbert and William Grant Still (4 each).

As can be seen from this list, composers of lighter or pop music, like Anderson, Rodgers, Romberg, and Herbert, compared well with composers of more "serious" concert music. Thus, in music of America as well as with music of Europe, conductors seemed to try to program things which have some familiarity for their audiences. This, together with the fact that many of the programs were a compromise between totally serious and lighter music, can explain the high incidence of lighter music as opposed to the serious composers' efforts.

The "familiarity factor" would explain why very little of any pop music of non-American contemporary composers was included: American conductors, by and large, are unacquainted with the lighter music being produced in Europe, and for community audiences it is a book with seven seals.

Orchestral materials for much of the lighter music performed are available for purchase by orchestras, whereas serious music of most American or non-American composers is available only on rental. When music of a lighter character is acquired through purchase, it is still subject to licensing agreements and the payment of performance royalties; one suspects, however, that many orchestras owning such materials conveniently or absentmindedly forget to pay the royalties.

How deeply the increasing rental and royalty fees charged by the publishers has affected the programming of serious contemporary music is a matter for speculation. Although it cannot be documented, informal discussions among conductors suggest this is a factor in programming.

Most of the titles of compositions played suggest a rather conservative approach to new music. This would seem to be a positive factor for most community orchestras. The most devout dedication to the latest advances in compositional styles is well and good, providing it doesn't drive both players and audience away.

No hard and fast rule can be given on how best to program contemporary music. Perhaps the best formula was stated by the conductor

James DePreist, who said, "If I don't feel a commitment to the composer and the work, I don't feel I can conduct it. I may be able to give it a creditable performance, but often with first hearings of new works that may be less accessible than most, creditable performances are not enough. What is needed is an inspired and dedicated performance."[4] Morton Gould summed up the predicament of the contemporary composer and symphony orchestras when he said at an American Symphony Orchestra League symposium, "Whether we like it or not, more people tend to come to hear Tchaikovsky than to hear a contemporary American composer. It's as simple and basic as that."[5]

SUMMARY

In summarizing the questionnaires and programs submitted, several observations may be noted: Orchestra programs tend to be somewhat conservative for community orchestras; there is a great reliance on the known works of any composer of any period; and conductors tend to program contemporary works which are lighter in character than companion works on the same program from earlier historical periods. These tendencies seem to correspond with the results of the more extensive surveys cited.

Programs of community orchestras, particularly regarding precontemporary retertoire, reflect the general trends of all orchestras, professional and semi-professional, as indicated in the BMI survey for 1969-70. We can tentatively assume that conductors, even when undergoing minimal pressure as to their choice of programs, will tend to select works generally considered "safe."

The general resurgence of interest in opera in the United States is also reflected in the programs of community orchestras.

Two questions were not answered because of the limited response: Are there geographical differences in programming policies, particularly regarding contemporary music? Do orchestras in isolated areas program differently from those community orchestras in metropolitan areas where one or more professional orchestras are performing regularly? The answers to these must await much additional information.

appendix A

Abstract of Internal Revenue Service Regulations Pertaining to Tax-Exempt Organizations

The following paragraphs are excerpted from Publication 557, United States Treasury Department, Bureau of Internal Revenue. Under most circumstances, only Chapters I and II of the publication apply to symphony orchestras. Orchestras wishing to acquire tax-exempt status would do well to review the entire publication, or discuss it with an officer of the Internal Revenue Service.

Chapter I — Procedures for Obtaining Recognition of Exemption

To qualify for exemption under the Internal Revenue Code you must be organized for one or more of the purposes specifically designated in the Code.

Application for tax exempt status must be filed with with District Director for the district in which the organization's principal office or place of business is located. If the application is submitted to the wrong office, it will be forwarded to the correct office and the applicant will be notified accordingly. The application will be referred by the district office where filed to one of 16 key Internal Revenue Service district offices for processing.

A ruling or determination letter will be issued in advance of operations if your organization can describe its proposed operations in sufficient detail to permit a conclusion that it will clearly meet the particular requirements of the section of law under which exemption is claimed.

The description of proposed operations must fully describe the activities in which the organization expects to engage, its expected sources of funds, and the nature of its contemplated expenditures.

With reference to expected sources of funds, it should be shown whether support will be from public or private sources. Also, the nature of the support should be explained, that is, whether contributions, grants or other form. If income from fund raising events, ticket sales, rentals, or other business or investment sources is anticipated, the nature of the venture or revenue-producing enterprise should be explained.

The nature of contemplated expenses should be shown.

Where an organization does not supply information of the nature discussed above, or fails to furnish a sufficiently detailed description of its proposed activities to permit a conclusion that it will clearly be exempt, a record of actual operations will be required before a ruling or determination letter is issued.

Most organizations seeking recognition of exemption must file an application on forms specifically prescribed by the Internal Revenue Service. These are Forms 1023, 1024, 1025, 1026 and 1027.

The purposes and proposed activities of your organization should be described in its articles of organization or other statements accompanying the application form. You should study the chapter in this publication that applies to your organization to determine the information to be provided.

Every exempt organization is required to have an Employer Identification Number, whether or not it has any employees. If your organization does not have an Employer Identification Number, your application for recognition of exemption should be accompanied by a completed Form SS-4, "Application for Employer Identification Number."

If your organization expects to be represented in person or by correspondence by an agent or attorney, you must file a power of attorney specifically authorizing the agent or attorney to represent your organization.

Oral requests for recognition of exemption will not be considered by the Internal Revenue Service.

An organization that is exempt from Federal Income tax other than as an organization described in section 501 (c) (3) of the Internal Revenue Code (see Chapter 2 of Publication 557) may, if it desires, establish a fund, separate and apart from its other funds, exclusively for religious, charitable, scientific, literary, or educational purposes or for the prevention of cruelty to children or animals.

[Author's note: This paragraph specifically allows the establishment of a separate fund within the orchestra's operations for scholarships for deserving younger musicians, or other purpose, provided that such fund is used for that purpose and not diverted to the general orchestra budget.]

If the fund is organized and operated exclusively for such purposes, it may qualify for exemption as an organization described in section 501 (c) (3) of the Internal Revenue Code, and contributions made to it will be deductible as provided by section 170 of the Internal Revenue Code. A fund of this character must be organized in such a manner as to prohibit the use of its funds upon dissolution, or otherwise, for the general purposes of the organization creating it.

Every organization exempt from Federal income tax under section 501 (c) (3) of the Code must file an annual information return on Form 990 except:

An organization (other than a private foundation) having gross receipts in each taxable year that are normally not more then $5000. The gross receipts of an organization are normally not more than $5000 if the average of the gross receipts received by the organization in the immediately preceding three years, including the year for which the return would be filed, is $5000 or less.

Chapter II — Charitable, Religious, Educational, Scientific Literary, etc., Organizations

An organization may qualify for exemption from Federal income tax if it is organized and operated exclusively for one or more of the following purposes: Charitable, Religious, Scientific, Testing for public safety, Literary, Educational or Prevention of cruelty to children or animals.

Form 1023 and accompanying statements must show that:
(1) The organization is organized exclusively for, and will be operated exclusively for, one or more of the purposes specified above;
(2) No part of its net earning will inure to the benefit of private shareholders or individuals; and
(3) It will not, as a substantial part of its activities, attempt to influence legislation, or participate to any extent in a political campaign for or against any candidate for public office.

[Author's note: Under the provisions of Tax Reform Act of 1976, Congress has provided an alternative to the "no substantial part" of 501 (c) (3) with a measurable standard which allows an organization, without jeopardy to its tax-exempt status, to expend a given percentage of its total annual budget for lobbying activities. Prior to the enactment of this Tax Reform of 1976, there was no yardstick by which to measure "substantial." Under the new guidelines, permissible percentages of total annual expenditures are:

Total Expenditures	Permissible Percentage
1st $500,000	20
2nd $500,000	15
3rd $500,000	10
Remaining expenditures	5

In addition to these overall limits on lobbying expenditures, a separate quantitative test is applied to so-called "grass roots" lobbying. This limit, which is 25% of the overall limit, applies to efforts aimed at procuring *public* support for a legislative position, while the basic limit applies to all expenses associated with legislative lobbying efforts.]

Your organization must include a confirmed copy of its articles of organization with the application for recognition of exemption. This may be its trust instrument, corporate charter, articles of association, or any other written instrument by which it is created.

Assets of an organization must be permanently dedicated to an exempt purpose. This means that should an organization dissolve, its assets will be distributed for an exempt purpose described in this chapter, or to the Federal Government or to a state or local government for a public purpose. If the assets could be distributed to members or private individuals for any other purpose, the organizational test is not met.

To establish that your organization's assets will be permanently dedicated to an exempt purpose, the articles of organization should contain a provision insuring their distribution for an exempt purpose in the event of dissolution. Although reliance may be placed upon state law to establish permanent dedication of assets for exempt purposes, your organization's application probably can be processed much more rapidly if its articles of organization include a provision insuring permanent dedication of assets for exempt purposes.

The term "educational" relates to the instruction or training of the individual for improving or developing his capabilities, or the instruction of the public on subjects useful to the individual and beneficial to the community.

The following types of organizations may qualify as educational: a museum, zoo, planetarium, symphony orchestra, or other similar organization.

[Author's note: There was a case where an agent of the Internal Revenue Service disallowed exemption for a symphony orchestra on the grounds that the orchestra in question did not program a "symphony" during the season. All other tests for exemption having been met, the orchestra won its case on appeal.]

appendix B

Suggestions for Audition Material

VIOLIN

Mozart, Overture to *The Marriage of Figaro.* Opening measures.
Brahms, Symphony No. 4 in E minor. Beginning of first movement.
Mozart, Symphony No. 40 in G minor. Fourth movement, at development.

VIOLA

Mozart, Symphony No. 40 in G minor. Opening measures.
Beethoven, Symphony No. 5 in C minor. Beginning of second movement.
Mozart, Overture to *The Marriage of Figaro.* Opening measures.

CELLO

Dvořák, Symphony No. 8 in G major. Beginning of last movement.
Mozart, Overture to *The Marriage of Figaro.* Opening measures.
Beethoven, Symphony No. 2 in D major. Opening of "Allegro con brio," after
  Introduction
Wagner, Prelude to *Tristan und Isolde.* Opening measures.

BASS

Beethoven, Symphony No. 8 in F major. Selected passages from first movement.
Brahms, Symphony No. 2 in D major. Second movement, beginning with the
  anacrusis to measure 23.
Brahms, *Academic Festival* Overture. Beginning measures.
Beethoven, Symphony No. 3 in Eb major. Scherzo.

FLUTE

Debussy, *Prelude a L'Apres midi d'un Faune.* Opening solo.
Brahms, Symphony No. 4 in E minor. Last movement, flute solo in 3/2 section.
Rimsky-Korsakov. *Russian Easter* Overture. Flute solos.
Beethoven, *Leonore* Overture No. 3.

OBOE

Rimsky-Korsakov, *Scheherazade.*
Oboe players should be able to give a good, steady concert "A," 440.
Beethoven, Symphony No. 5 in C minor. Cadenza in first movement.
Brahms, Violin Concerto in D major. Solo in second movement.

CLARINET

Mozart, Clarinet Concerto in A. Selected passages.
Brahms, Symphony No. 2 in D major. Trio to the third movement.

BASSOON

Tchaikovsky, Symphony No. 5 in E minor. Third movement.
Beethoven, Symphony No. 8 in F major. Fourth movement.
Haydn, Symphony No. 88 in G major. Fourth movement.

HORN

Tchaikovsky, Symphony No. 5 in E minor. Solo in second movement.
Brahms, Symphony No. 2 in D major. Fanfare at end of last movement.
Beethoven, Symphony No. 8 in F major. Trio section of Scherzo.

TRUMPET

Rimsky-Korsakov, Suite from *L'Coq d'Or.* Opening solo.
Dvořák, Symphony No. 8 in G major. Last movement, opening.
Brahms, Symphony No. 2 in D major. Closing measures of last movement.
Gounod, *Faust* Ballet Music. Solo in next to last movement.

TROMBONE

Mozart, *Requiem Mass.* "Tuba mirum" solo.
Berlioz, "Rakoczy" March.
Brahms, Symphony No. 1 in C minor. Chorale from fourth movement.
Rimsky-Korsakov, *Russian Easter* Overture. Trombone solos.

TUBA

Prokofiev, *Lt. Kije.* Third movement, "Kije's Wedding."
Shostakovich, Symphony No. 5. Last movement.

HARP

Rimsky-Korsakov, *Capriccio Espagnol.* Harp cadenza.
Tchaikovsky, "Nutcracker" Ballet. Harp cadenza.
Tchaikovsky, *Swan Lake* harp parts.
Franck, Symphony in D minor. Harp part for second movement.

PIANO AND CELESTE

Shostakovich, Symphony No. 5. First and last movements (piano).
Copland, *El Salon Mexico.* Piano parts throughout.
Mozart, *Magic Flute.* Celeste solos.

PERCUSSION

Morris Goldenberg, *The Modern School of Snare Drumming.* Chapple and Company, Inc. All exercises through page 23. Also, the roll exercises on page 44. The community orchestra percussionist ought to be able to perform on a variety of percussion instruments.

Anthony J. Cirone, *Portraits in Rhythm.* Belwin Music, Inc. First etude.

For mallet percussion instruments, the ability to perform the top voice of either the F major or D minor *Two-Part Inventions* by Bach.

For timpani, audition material can be found in the *Ludwig Drum Instructor*, William F. Ludwig Co., Chicago, Illinois.

Also, the prospective timpanist should be able to tune the drums accurately.

appendix C

Useful Addresses

I. *RENTAL LIBRARIES*

American Composers' Alliance, 170 W. 74th Street, New York, New York 10023.

American Music Center, 250 W. 57th Street, New York, New York 10019.

S. Eugene Bailey, 217 Union Street, Northfield, Minnesota 55057.
> The Bailey catalogue has many standard items together with some works not generally found in some larger catalogues.

The Fleischer Collection of the Free Library of Philadelphia, Logan Square, Philadelphia, Pennsylvania 19103.
> This library will loan, free of charge except for postage, items which are not found in the commercial libraries. If a conductor cannot locate a work anywhere else, the Library may have it or will provide information about where it may be found.

James K. Guthrie, Music Librarian, 3275 Valencia Avenue, San Bernardino, California 92404.
> Mr. Guthrie advertises "super-fast" service. His library incorporates the materials in the former James Dolan collection as well as many new additions. Mr. Guthrie also will provide special arrangements, put in bowings and cuts when desired.

Luck's Music Library, 15701 E. Warren, Detroit, Michigan 48224.
> Mostly standard works are found in Luck's catalogues. This company specializes in very fast and economical service.

Mapleson's Music Library, 110 W. 40th Street, New York, New York, 10018.
> Mapleson has the largest collection of orchestral materials for stage works, including almost all of the Gilbert and Sullivan works.

II. *PUBLISHERS*

Most publishers' catalogues provide information as to whether a work may be purchased or if it is available only on rental.

Associated Music Publishers. Now merged with G. Schirmer, Inc.

Belwin-Mills, Inc., 25 Deshon Avenue, Melville, New York 11746.
Belwin is the agent for Ricordi and many other European publishing houses, as well as publishing much contemporary American music under its own name.

Boosey & Hawkes, Inc., Oceanside, New York 11562.
Material of Britten, Richard Strauss, Copland and many others is available only from Boosey & Hawkes. In addition, they are the agents for several European publishing houses.

Alexander Broude, Inc., 225 W. 57th Street, New York, New York 10019.
Broude has a good collection of standard materials as well as some imported items from Europe which are hard to find elsewhere.

Broude Brothers, Inc., 56 W. 45th Street, New York, New York 10036.
Broude Brothers has a very large collection of scores and parts available for sale. In addition, they publish the Rongwen Edition of contemporary orchestral music.

Chappel Music Co., Inc., 810 Seventh Avenue, New York, New York 10019.

Drinker Choral Library, The Free Library, Logan Square, Philadelphia, Pennsylvania 19103.
This is the library arm of the American Choral Society.
Groups belonging to the Society can borrow multiple copies of a large collection of choral works. Rental charge is for postage only.

Elkan-Vogel Company, c/o Theodore Presser Company, Presser Place, Bryn Mawr, Pennsylvania 19010. Elkan-Vogel publishes several American composers as well as being American agents for several French publishers.

European-American Music Distributor Corp., 195 Allwood Road, Clifton, New Jersey 07012; formerly Joseph Boonin, Inc.
New American agent for Universal Edition, B. Schott, and others.

Carl Fischer, Inc., 62 Cooper Square, New York, New York 10003.
Fischer has a catalogue of standard materials as well as publishing several contemporary American composers.

Galaxy Music Corporation, 2121 Broadway, New York, New York 10023.
Publishes several American composers both under its own name and that of its subsidiary, Highgate Press. Galaxy is also the American agent for Augener and Joseph Williams of England.

International Music Company, 511-5th Avenue, New York, New York 10017.
Orchestral catalogue is small, but contains some items not to be found elsewhere.

Edwin F. Kalmus, P.O. Box 1007, Opa-locka, Florida 33054.
  Kalmus deals in his own reprints. Some of the material is quite good, but the conductor must guard against errors in parts.

Music Corporation of America (MCA Music), c/o Belwin-Mills, Inc., 25 Deshon Avenue, Melville, New York 11746. Agents for Leeds, Inc., publishers of most composers from the Soviet Union.

Oxford University Press, Inc., 200 Madison Avenue, New York, New York 10016.
  Oxford publishes the music of Vaughan Williams and William Walton as well as many other English composers.

C. F. Peters Corporation, 373 Park Avenue South, New York, New York 10016.
  Publisher of several American composers, most notably Alan Hovhaness. Their catalogue has a good collection of Baroque works in performing editions.

Theodore Presser Company, Presser Place, Bryn Mawr, Pennsylvania 19010.
  Presser publishes many American composers as well as serving as agent for several European publishers.

Editions Salabert, 575 Madison Avenue, New York, New York 10022. Agents and publishers for many French composers.

G. Schirmer, Inc., 866 Third Avenue, New York, New York 10022.
  With its merger with Associated Music Publishers, Schirmer has become one of the largest publishing houses in the country. Much contemporary American music is available from here as well as a large selection of standard works.

Shawnee Press, Inc., Delaware Water Gap, Pennsylvania 18327.

Southern Music Publishing Co., 1740 Broadway, New York, New York 10019.

Tams-Witmark Music Library, 115-117 W. 45th Street, New York, New York 10036.
  Conductors looking for complete materials for Broadway musicals should consult Tams-Witmark catalogue.

III. *SERVICE, LICENSING AND MISCELLANEOUS ORGANIZATIONS*

American Society of Composers, Authors and Publishers (ASCAP), 1 Lincoln Plaza, New York, New York 10023.
  Information on licensing agreements as well as much information on American composers may be obtained from ASCAP.

American Symphony Orchestra League, Inc., P.O. Box 66, Vienna, Virginia 22180.
  The service organization for symphony orchestras. The League also publishes several handbooks and other materials covering many facets of orchestra operations. Conductors and managers may receive information on job openings from the League for an additional membership fee.

Broadcast Music, Inc. (BMI), 40 W. 57th Street, New York, New York 10019.
  BMI publishes brochures on many composers, can provide information on

licensing agreements, and provide much information on American composers and their music.

Leonard Burkat Program Note Service, 563 Branchville Road, Ridgefield, Connecticut 06877.

Program notes prepared and delivered at reasonable cost. Special rush order service available if needed. (Founded by Paul Affelder.)

Central Opera Service, Metropolitan Opera House, Lincoln Plaza, New York, New York 10023.

COS membership is very informative for the conductor involved in opera production. The Service publishes, in addition to its *Bulletin*, lists of costume rental agencies, information about location of opera sets available for rental, and other useful data.

Thea Dispeker Artists' Representative, 59 E. 54th Street, New York, New York 10022.

This agency is the representative in charge of booking engagements for the annual Leventritt Foundation artists.

International Contemporary Music Exchange, 58 W. 58th Street, Suite 29B, New York, New York 10019.

Musical America-Hi Fidelity Publications, 165 W. 46th Street, New York, New York 10036.

The annual Directory Issue of *Musical America* provides information about orchestras and their seasons, together with advertisements from all artists' managers, large and small. Conductors interested in engaging "name" soloists should consult this Directory Issue.

Wenger Corporation, 573 Park Drive, Owatonna, Minnesota 55069.

Wenger constructs standard and custom orchestra shells, risers, and portable stages as well as many other useful items for music rooms and auditoria.

appendix D

Orchestras and Conductors Returning Questionnaires and Submitting Programs

Arlington Symphony, Arlington, Virginia. Karl Rucht, Conductor.

Bremerton Symphony, Bremerton, Washington. David Avshalomov, Conductor.

Brevard Symphony Orchestra, Cocoa, Florida. Joseph Kreines, Conductor.

Cape Cod Symphony Orchestra, Barnstable, Massachusetts. Jerome D. Cohen, Conductor.

Champaign-Urbana Symphony, Champaign, Illinois. Bernard Goodman, Conductor.

Fort Myers Symphony Orchestra and Opera Association. Arlo C. I. Daibler, Conductor.

Haddonfield Symphony Society, Haddonfield, New Jersey. Arthur Cohn, Conductor.

Hamilton Symphony Orchestra, Hamilton, Ohio. Robert Martin, Conductor.

Johnstown Symphony Orchestra, Johnstown, Pennsylvania. Dr. Michael Semanitzky, Conductor.

Lakeland Symphony Orchestra, Lakeland, Florida. Jay W. Erwin, Conductor.

Lima Symphony Orchestra, Lima, Ohio. Joseph Firszt, Conductor.

Magic Valley Symphony, Twin Falls, Idaho. Del Slaughter, Conductor.

Minot Symphony Orchestra, Minot, North Dakota. Jerold A. Sundet, Conductor.

New Hampshire Music Festival, Center Harbor, New Hampshire. Thomas Nee, Conductor.

Port Angeles Symphony Orchestra, Port Angeles, Washington. James Van Horn, Conductor.

Rockford Symphony Orchestra, Rockford, Illinois. Crawford Gates, Conductor.

Sioux City Symphony Orchestra, Sioux City, Iowa. Leo Kucinski, conductor.

Spartanburg Symphony Orchestra. Spartanburg, South Carolina Henry Janiec, Conductor.

Terre Haute Symphony, Terre Haute, Indiana. Dr. Victor B. Denek, Conductor.

West Suburban Symphony Orchestra, La Grange, Illinois. Irwin Fischer, Conductor.

One orchestra returned a questionnaire, but did not identify itself or its conductor.

Although the formal questionnaire was not returned, the late LeRoy Anderson, composer and manager of the Waterbury Symphony Orchestra in Connecticut, wrote the author a long letter commenting on the questionnaire.

Not all orchestras responding submitted both questionnaire and programs: several orchestras or conductors returned questionnaire with no programs, and two groups of programs were sent with no questionnaire response.

appendix E

The Conductors' Guild

In June of 1974, at the American Symphony Orchestra League's National Conference in Memphis, Tennessee, several conductors gathered together to discuss informally problems germane to conductors. Out of those discussions was born the Conductors' Guild. During the year that followed, ground work to establish a meaningful organization *for* conductors which would be run *by* conductors was begun.

At the 1975 League Conference in San Diego, a slate of candidates was put before the attending conductors and the first Conductors' Guild officers and board members were elected. At that time, each board member and several appointed committee members were given the specific assignment to investigate one area of interest or concern to conductors and communicate the findings in a paper. It was the Guild's intent to have those papers read at the 1976 conference and to place a synopsis of each paper in the hands of all member conductors for their personal use. The papers dealt with such areas of interest as the conductor's relationship to managers, unions, critics, the International Congress of Symphony and Opera Musicians (I.C.S.O.M.), orchestra committees, symphony boards, and audition procedures. There were also studies of foreign conductors on American podiums, conducting competitions in the United States, recordings, conductor contracts, etc.

During the 1976 League Conference in Boston, the Conductors' Guild held its first official meetings. The assembled conductors elected three new board members, heard the reading of most of the aforementioned position papers and studies, approved a set of By-laws, and sponsored two sessions of live symphonic music, a practice which had all but disappeared from League conferences for many years.

While in Boston, members of the executive board of the Guild met with the chairperson of I.C.S.O.M. and two Boston Symphony I.C.S.O.M. representatives to discuss mutual concerns. Following this discussion, three Guild board members were invited to attend the I.C.S.O.M. national conference in Denver the following August. Dialogue between the two organizations continues. At issue between the two organizations has been and is the use of conductor evaluation questionnaires and the feeling on the part of the Guild that in some instances these have been used improperly, to the detriment of certain conductors.

During the 1976-77 season, the Guild sent to all member conductors copies of its Bylaws together with synopses of several papers read in Boston. Since the Guild is affiliated with the League, the Chairperson of the Guild Executive Board sits as a member of the League Board of Directors. In addition, there are several other conductors who are members of the League board.

The Conductors' Guild presently represents a strong moral and professional force that is addressing itself to the problems and aspirations of American conductors. All conductors are urged to become involved with the Guild. For the benefit of conductors, managers and board members, here follows the Conductors' Guild paper on conductor contracts written by Emerson Buckley, Music Director of the Fort Lauderdale (Florida) Symphony. The sources for this paper were contracts from various music directors in all orchestra categories. The author is personally indebted to Mr. Buckley for his gracious permission to use his paper in this volume. While each orchestra is unique and no survey can adequately cover every contingency, special problems within each situation will require identification and a mutually agreeable solution. It is to be understood that much of the wording in this paper assumes a totally union orchestra; in the case of community orchestras, some of the references to the American Federation of Musicians are unnecessary. (The word "association" in the paper that follows refers to the governing body of the orchestra.)

Basic Contractual Information

ENGAGEMENT

The contract begins by clearly stating that Maestro ____ is being engaged by the "____ Symphony Orchestra" for the period commencing (date) and concluding (date) . These dates should run concurrent with the orchestra's *fiscal* year and *not* with the calendar year. (The June 1-May 31 fiscal year affords the advantage of concluding the year's business in May thus making the summer period, Memorial Day to Labor Day, more available for summer guest appearances by the conductor).

SUMMER ABSENCE

Some associations insert a contractual clause permitting the conductor to absent himself entirely from local activities for three months (June, July and August unless otherwise specified in the original employment dates) for guest engagements, or study. Under such an arrangement the association could ask to have the conductor return for concert or consultation by paying his round-trip travel expenses.

FIRST CONTRACT

If the conductor, new to the area, accepts a first contract and is expected to reside in a new location, compensation for a move to the orchestra's city should be given by the association if the move is in excess of 50 miles.

MUSICAL DUTIES

Maestro ___ agrees to supervise, prepare, program, rehearse and conduct (specify number) subscription (or series) concerts given by the "___ Symphony Orchestra": in the (local) area under the jurisdiction of local (XYZ) of the American Federation of Musicians during the seasons to run approximately from September (October) to May (June) of each year. (If possible the specific concert dates should be included. This information is normally available one, sometimes two full years in advance).

In the event the number of concerts on the subscription series is augmented *after* the contract has been signed the clause "(number) subscription concerts . . . in the (local) area" would allow the conductor to negotiate remuneration for the additional concerts should he wish to do so. The conductor agrees to devote his time and conscientious efforts to the overall artistic direction and public promotion *whenever feasible* of the orchestra for the life of the contract. The Musical Division agrees to perform said musical duties within budgeting guidelines established in the association's budget.

MUSICIANS — (SOLOISTS — PROGRAMS)

The sole responsibility for the hiring and firing of orchestra musicians (and choosing of soloists and programs) rests with the conductor.

The personnel manager (contractor) will be a person mutually agreeable to himself and management. The conductor should warrant that he is or will become a member of the local AFM and will remain so for the duration of the contract.

ASSOCIATION MUSIC COMMITTEE

If a music committee or artistic advisory committee exists within the association, the conductor should submit to this committee tentative programs for the coming season on or before a mutually agreed-to date. The conductor should be receptive to the subsequent suggestions and recommendations of the committee, but retains *final* artistic decision-making in the areas of programming and soloists.

Due to problems of bookings, the music committee should secure from the executive or budget committee an allocation for guest artists *before* the final fiscal year budget is set. (December 1 of the previous season is none too early.)

SALARY

The conductor's salary must be clearly stated on an annual basis conforming to the exact dates of the contract. A schedule of monthly or semi-monthly payments should also be set forth.

For example, the clause could read "The conductor's salary for the fiscal year 1976-77 will be in the amount of *$XXX*. Twelve monthly (or 24 semi-monthly) payments will be made in the amount of *$XXX* per payment to be received by the conductor on or before the first (and/or 15th) day of each month, such payments to begin on (date) 1977." This format should be repeated using new figures if the conductor is signing a two-year contract in which the second year's salary will be higher than the first.

To grant the conductor some degree of privacy regarding his salary, the association should combine his salary with another line item in the annual budget. Line items for soloists, musicians or artistic personnel can be used. Only appropriate association members should be cognizant of the figure.

MEDICAL INSURANCE

It is advisable that the association supply major medical insurance for conductor and family.

SOCIAL SECURITY

If social security is not paid, an annuity equal in cost to the social security payments should be established.

PENSION

It is advisable that the association provide the conductor with enrollment in a pension plan such as that offered by the A.S.O.L.

EXPENSE ACCOUNT

It is advisable to include an expense account for Musical Director within the budget. However, if a music director does not have a budgeted expense account, a clause should be placed into the contract which would provide for the reimbursement of monies spent by him for activities defined and agreed upon by the smallest possible number of association personnel.

OUTSIDE ENGAGEMENTS

The association agrees to allow the conductor to participate in guest engagements with other organizations producing concerts, opera, ballet, recordings, radio, T.V., etc., in any part of the world on dates that are "mutually agreed upon with management" as long as the artistic standards of the association are upheld. (For efficient interaction between the conductor and the association, the word "management" when used contractually should represent the smallest number of people possible).

The conductor should be permitted to act in any executive or instructional capacity with an academic institution. He should be allowed time for private teaching, composing, writing, etc. If the conductor has a full- or part-time position with another artistic organization, especially if that organization is under the jurisdiction of the same Local of the A.F. of M. as the association, the position should be mentioned by name and a contractual right of retention should be inserted.

GUEST CONDUCTING

The association should encourage outside guest engagements for its conductor. The orchestra derives obvious benefits from such an arrangement. In a season series of eight or more concerts it is probable that the association will want to use one or two guest conductors. In a series of twelve or more concerts, two or three guest conductors could be used. Both the association and the conductor should strive to secure guest conductors who would enhance the series.

SPECIAL NOTE: Guest Appearances

Very often the contract for a guest appearance will include a clause stating that the "conductor will rehearse from a schedule supplied by the management." Such a clause is usually readily agreed to by the artist's representative. To protect the artistic excellence of the performance, a guest conductor should secure *in writing* an agreement governing the *minimum* orchestra-rehearsal time. This is especially important in the areas of opera or oratorio productions. Such an agreement will allow the guest conductor to make an educated guess as to whether or not the allotted rehearsal time is sufficient to produce the minimum artistic standards that the conductor's integrity will allow.

PUBLICITY

The association should agree that whenever the orchestra's name is used officially, especially in promotional material, the name of the conductor will also appear. The conductor should retain control over the use of the term "members of" the orchestra as well as the use of his own name in such situations.

RECORDINGS

The conductor should not allow radio, T.V. or tape recordings of association concerts unless agreed to in advance, in writing. The conductor should reserve the right to veto transmission of any tape, video or audio if the results do not meet his artistic standards. (Commercial transmission of performances should result in compensation of both the conductor and the orchestra's musicians.)

RENEWAL—NON-RENEWAL

A date on which the association would commence deliberations for renewal or non-renewal of the conductor's contract should be specified. A consummation date no later than *one year before* the expiration of the present contract should be selected and mutually agreed upon. The contract should be signed by the association's President and Executive Vice-President and counter-signed by the conductor under an "agreed to and accepted" clause at the end of the contract.

LEGAL ADVICE

All contracts should be written and/or scrutinized by an attorney. It might be advisable to have your personal representative and an attorney collaborate on the consummation of the contract. Both parties should strive for a clear, readable contract. Ambiguity that could result in confusion should be eliminated. Brevity can often be the best ally of clarity.

Notes

CHAPTER 1

1. Helen M. Thompson, *The Community Symphony Orchestra—How to Organize and Develop It* (Charleston, W.V.: The American Symphony Orchestra League, Inc., 1952), p. 20.
2. Thompson, *Community Symphony Orchestra*, p. 49.
3. Thompson, *Community Symphony Orchestra*, p. 19.
4. Helen M. Thompson's *Report of Study on Governing Boards of Symphony Orchestras* (Charleston, W.V.: American Symphony Orchestra League, 1958) and *Study of Legal Documents of Symphony Orchestras* (Charleston, West Virginia: American Symphony Orchestra League, 1958) are available from the American Symphony Orchestra League, P. O. Box 669, Vienna, Virginia 22180. The *Study* presents several model documents, all of which fulfill the requirements of the Internal Revenue Service code. New orchestras would be well advised to model their official documents after one or more of those contained in this *Study*.
5. Thompson, *Community Symphony Orchestra*, p. 59.
6. Thompson, *Community Symphony Orchestra*, p. 52.
7. Thompson, *Community Symphony Orchestra*, p. 52.

CHAPTER 2

1. William J. Baumol, and William G. Bowen, *Performing Arts, The Economic Dilemma* (New York: Twentieth Century Fund, 1966), p. 332.
2. Alvin Toffler, *The Culture Consumers* (New York: St. Martin's Press, 1964), p. 94.
3. Baumol and Bowen, *Performing Arts*, p. 345.
4. Julius Novick, *Beyond Broadway: The Quest for Permanent Theatres* (New York: Hill and Wang, 1968), p. 6.
5. Toffler, *Culture Consumers*, p. 32.

6. Baumol and Bowen, *Performing Arts*, p. 80.

7. Toffler, *Culture Consumers*, p. 110.

8. Baumol and Bowen, *Performing Arts*, p. 327.

9. Leslie C. White, and Helen M. Thompson, eds., *Survey of Arts Councils* (Charleston, W.V.: American Symphony Orchestra League, 1959).

CHAPTER 3

1. Instrumental Music, Inc., 1416 Lake Street, Evanston, Ill. 62205, and Gamble Hinged Music Company, 312 Wabash Avenue, Chicago, Ill. 60604 are two supply houses from which library supplies are available. (Experience has shown that with orchestral music, the closed end of these boxes should be sealed with a heavy-duty filament tape. The cardboard used is not of sufficient strength to stand repeated openings. It is also advisable to put a heavy-duty rubber band around the boxes.

2. Charles L. Gary, ed., *Music Buildings, Rooms and Equipment* (Washington, D.C.: Music Educators National Conference, 1966), contains specific comments concerning acoustics beginning with page 60.

3. Gary, *Music Buildings*, p. 47.

4. Gary, *Music Buildings*, pp. 49-59 contain suggestions regarding stage and pit areas.

5. Gary, *Music Buildings*, p. 60.

CHAPTER 4

1. Quoted in Carl Bamberger, *The Conductor's Art* (New York: McGraw-Hill, 1965), pp. 22-23.

2. Quoted in Bamberger, *Conductor's Art*, p. 312.

3. In Herbert Kupferberg, *Those Fabulous Philadelphians* (New York: Charles Scribner's Sons, 1969), p. 191.

4. Bamberger, *Conductor's Art*, p. 3.

5. Quoted in Bamberger, *Conductor's Art*, p. 202.

6. Hermann Scherchen, *Handbook of Conducting*, trans. M. D. Calvocoressi (London: Oxford University Press, 1933), p. 4.

7. Scherchen, *Handbook of Conducting*, p. 14.

8. Scherchen, *Handbook of Conducting*, pp. 188-89.

9. Quoted in Bamberger, *Conductor's Art*, p. 45.

10. Quoted in Bamberger, *Conductor's Art*, p. 117.

11. Quoted in Bamberger, *Conductor's Art*, p. 74.

12. Quoted in Bamberger, *Conductor's Art*, p. 211.

13. Quoted in Bamberger, *Conductor's Art*, p. 272.

14. Quoted in Bamberger, *Conductor's Art*, p. 226.

15. Quoted in Bamberger, *Conductor's Art*, p. 243.

16. Quoted in Bamberger, *Conductor's Art*, p. 110.

17. Quoted in Bamberger, *Conductor's Art*, p. 113-14.

18. Quoted in Bamberger, *Conductor's Art*, p. 150.

19. Malcolm H. Holmes, *Conducting an Amateur Orchestra* (Cambridge: Harvard University Press, 1951), p. 3.

20. Lloyd Pfautsch, "The Choral Conductor and the Rehearsal," in Harold A. Decker, and Julius Herford, *Choral Conducting: A Symposium* (Englewood Cliffs, N.J.: Prentice-Hall, Inc., 1973), p. 58.

21. Daniel Moe, "The Choral Conductor and Twentieth Century Choral Music," in Decker and Herford, *Choral Conducting*, p. 157.

22. Quoted in Hubert Roussel, *The Houston Symphony Orchestra, 1913-1971* (Austin: University of Texas Press, 1972), p. 195.

23. Pfautsch, "The Choral Conductor," p. 59.

24. D. E. Inghelbrecht, *The Conductor's World*, trans. G. Prebauer and S. Malcolm Kirk (New York: Library Publishers, 1954), p. 6.

25. Quoted in Bamberger, *Conductor's Art*, p. 274.

26. William J. Finn, *The Conductor Raises His Baton* (London: Dennis Dobson Ltd., 1947), p. 7.

27. Erwin Stein, *Form and Performance* (London: Faber and Faber, [1962]), p. 11.

28. Inghelbrecht, *Conductor's World*, pp. 15-16.

CHAPTER 5

1. Malcolm H. Holmes, *Conducting an Amateur Orchestra*, (Cambridge: Harvard University Press, 1951), pp. 20-21.

2. Holmes, *Amateur Orchestra*, p. 14.

3. Holmes, *Amateur Orchestra*, p. 80.

CHAPTER 6

1. In an interview in *Time*, 4 January 1954, p. 48.

2. In a private comment to the author in 1954.

3. Daniel Moe, "The Choral Conductor and Twentieth Century Choral Music," in Harold Decker and Julius Herford, *Choral Conducting: A Symposium* (Englewood Cliffs, N.J.: Prentice-Hall, Inc., 1973), p. 142.

4. Central Opera Service, Metropolitan Opera House, Lincoln Center Plaza, New York, N.Y. 10023.

CHAPTER 7

1. John K. Sherman, *Music and Maestros: The Story of the Minneapolis Symphony Orchestra* (Minneapolis: University of Minnesota Press, 1952), p. 173.

2. Sherman, *Music and Maestros*, p. 172.

CHAPTER 8

1. James G. Roy, Jr., ed., *BMI Orchestral Program Survey, 1969–70 Concert Season* (New York: Broadcast Music, Inc., 1970).

2. Philip Hart, *Orpheus in the New World: The Symphony Orchestra as an American Cultural Institution* (New York: W. W. Norton & Co., 1973), p. 416.

3. Oliver Daniel in the Preface to *BMI Survey*.

4. Quoted in *Symphony News* 24, no. 5 (October-November 1973), p. 14.

5. *Symphony News*, 24, no. 5 (October–November 1973), p. 12.

Bibliography

The Bibliography is a selected list of materials to which the community orchestra conductor might wish to refer. The author assumes that the conductor is a conversant with the standard musical reference works such as Baker's *Biographical Dictionary* and the Grove's *Dictionary of Music and Musicians*. These and other standard reference works can provide much useful information in writing program notes, press releases, and preparing layout work on programs.

The ASCAP Biographical Dictionary of Composers, Authors and Publishers. New York: American Society of Composers, Authors, and Publishers, 1966.

American Symphony Orchestra League Resource Guide. Vienna, Virginia: American Symphony Orchestra League, 1977. (Updated periodically)

American Symphony Orchestra League. *Fund-Raising Projects of Symphony Women's Associations.* 1974-75 Season. Vienna, Virginia: American Symphony Orchestra League, 1975. (Updated periodically)

American Symphony Orchestra League. *Study of Legal Documents of Symphony Orchestras.* Charleston, West Virginia: The American Symphony Orchestra League, Inc., 1958.

Bamberger, Carl, ed. *The Conductor's Art.* New York: McGraw-Hill, 1965.

Baumol, William J., and William G. Bowen. *Performing Arts, The Economic Dilemma.* New York: The Twentieth-Century Fund, 1966.

Berglund, Don. "A Study of the Life and Work of Frederick Stock." Ph.D. dissertation, Northwestern University, 1955.

Berlioz, Hector. *Treatise on Instrumentation.* Edited and revised by Richard Strauss, translated by Theo. Front. New York: Edwin F. Kalmus, 1948.

Boult, Sir Adrian. *A Handbook on the Technique of Conducting.* Oxford: Hall, 1936.

Boult, Sir Adrian. *Thoughts on Conducting.* London: Phoenix House, 1963.

Bowles, Michael. *The Art of Conducting.* Garden City, New York: Doubleday, 1959.

Braithwaite, Warwick. *The Conductor's Art.* New York: John de Graff, Inc., 1952.

Chase, Gilbert, ed. *The American Composer Speaks: A Historical Anthology, 1770–1965.* Baton Rouge: Louisiana State University Press, 1966.

Cormier, Richard E. "The Founding of the St. Joseph Symphony Orchestra and Its Effects on School and Community." Ed.D. dissertation, Columbia University, 1964.

Decker, Harold A., and Julius Herford. *Choral Conducting: A Symposium.* Englewood Cliffs, New Jersey: Prentice-Hall, Inc., 1973.

Erhart, Will. *The Eloquent Baton.* New York: Witmark, 1931.

Finn, William J. *The Conductor Raises His Baton.* London: Dennis Dobson, Ltd., 1946.

Fott, Solie, "The Youth Education Activities of the Nashville Symphony Association." Ph.D. dissertation, George Peabody College for Teachers, 1958.

Galkin, Elliott W. "Theory and Practice of Conducting Since 1752." Ph.D. dissertation, Cornell University, 1960.

Gary, Charles L., ed. *Music Buildings, Rooms and Equipment.* Washington, D.C.: Music Educators National Conference, 1966.

Getchell, Robert W. "An Investigation of, and Recommendations for the Beginning Conducting Class in the College Curriculum." Ph.D. dissertation, State University of Iowa, 1957.

Gilman, Lawrence. *Orchestral Music: An Armchair Guide.* Edited by Edward Cushing. New York: Oxford University Press, 1951.

Goldbeck, Frederick. *The Perfect Conductor.* New York: Pellegrini, 1951.

Goodman, Alvin. "Development of the Symphony Orchestra in Higher Education." Ed.D. dissertation, University of Southern California, 1960.

Green, Elizabeth. *The Modern Conductor.* Englewood Cliffs, New Jersey: Prentice-Hall, 1961. 2nd Edition, 1973.

Grosbayne, Benjamin. *Techniques of Modern Orchestral Conducting.* Cambridge: Harvard University Press, 1956.

Hart, Philip. *Orpheus in the New World: The Symphony Orchestra as an American Cultural Institution.* New York: W.W. Norton & Co., 1973.

Hill, Thomas H., and Helen M. Thompson. *The Organization, Administration and Presentation of Symphony Orchestra Youth Concert Activities for Music Educational Purpose in Selected Cities.* Washington, D.C.: Bureau of Research, Office of Education, U.S. Department of Health, Education and Welfare, January 1968.

Holmes, Malcolm. *Conducting an Amateur Orchestra.* Cambridge: Harvard University Press, 1951.

Inghelbrecht, D.E. *The Conductor's World.* Translated by G. Prebauer and S. Malcolm Kirk. New York: Library Publishers, 1954.

Kaplan, Abraham. *Choral Conducting Manual.* New York: Macmillan, forthcoming.

Korman, Bernard. "Performance Rights in Music under Sections 110 and 118 of the 1976 Copyright Act." *New York Law School Law Review* XXII, No. 3 (1977). (Available in Reprint from ASCAP)

Krone, Max Thomas. *Expressive Conducting.* Rev. ed. Chicago: Kjos, 1949.

Krueger, Karl. *The Way of the Conductor, His Origins, Purpose, and Procedures.* New York: Charles Scribner's Sons, 1958.

Krueger, Richard R., trans. "Weingartner's Suggestions for the Performance of the Symphonies of Schubert and Schumann." D.M.A. dissertation, University of Washington, 1970.

Kupferberg, Herbert. *Those Fabulous Philadelphians.* New York: Charles Scribner's Sons, 1969.

Leichtentritt, Hugo. *Serge Koussevitsky and the Boston Symphony Orchestra.* Cambridge: Harvard University Press, 1946.

Lewis, L. Rhodes. "A Study of 15 Selected Community Orchestras in the United States." Ph.D. dissertation, State University of Iowa, 1956.

Leyden, Norman. "A Study and Analysis of the Conducting Patterns of Arturo Toscanini as Demonstrated in Minescope Films." Ed.D. dissertation, Columbia University, 1968.

McElheran, Brock. *Conducting Technique for Beginners and Professionals.* New York: Oxford University Press, 1966.

McNaughton, Charles D. "Albert Stoessel, American Musician." Ph.D. dissertation, New York University, 1957.

Mattheson, Johann. *Der vollkommene Capellmeister, 1739.* Kassel, Bärenreiter, 1954.

Melendy, Earle R. "The Development of Selected College and University Orchestras in the United States." Ed.D. dissertation, University of Virginia, 1955.

Mueller, Kate Hevner. *Twenty-seven Major Orchestras.* Bloomington: University of Indiana Press, 1973.

Nelms, William. *A Guide to Accounting Procedures and Record Keeping for Community Symphony Orchestras.* Vienna, Virginia: American Symphony Orchestra League, 1965.

Novick, Julius. *Beyond Broadway, the Quest for Permanent Theatres.* New York: Hill and Wang, 1968.

Paulakis, Christopher. *The American Music Handbook.* New York: The Free Press, 1974.

Pearsall, Howard T. "The North Carolina Symphony Orchestra from 1932 to 1962: Its Founding, Musical Growth, and Musical Activities." Mus. Ed.D. dissertation, Indiana University, 1969.

Poggi, Jack. *Theater in America: The Impact of Economic Forces, 1870–1967.* Ithaca, New York: Cornell University Press, 1968.

Rabin, Marvin. "History and Analysis of the Greater Boston Youth Symphony Orchestra from 1958 to 1964." Ed.D. dissertation, University of Illinois, 1968.

Raleigh, Elizabeth Ann. "Planning and the Performing Arts." University of Washington Master of Business Administration research report, University of Washington, 1975.

Rich, Maria F., ed. *Opera Repertory U.S.A. 1966–1972.* New York: Central Opera Service Bulletin, Winter 1972-73.

Rockefeller Panel Report. *The Performing Arts: Problems and Prospects.* New York: McGraw-Hill, 1965.

Roussel, Hubert. *The Houston Symphony Orchestra, 1913–1971.* Austin, Texas:

University of Texas Press, 1972.

Roy, James G. Jr., ed. *BMI Orchestral Program Survey, 1969–70 Concert Season.* New York: Broadcast Music, Inc., 1970.

Rudolf, Max. *The Grammar of Conducting.* New York: G. Schirmer, 1950.

Scherchen, Hermann. *Handbook of Conducting.* Translated by M.D. Calvocoressi. London: Oxford University Press, 1933.

Schickel, Richard. *The Arts: The Creative Individual and the Community: A Growing Collaboration.* New York: The Rockefeller Foundation, n.d.

Schwann Catalogue of Records and Tapes I, December 1973. Boston: W. Schwann, Inc., 1973.

Stein, Erwin. *Form and Performance.* London: Faber & Faber, 1962.

Sherman, John K. *Music and Maestros: The Story of the Minneapolis Symphony Orchestra.* Minneapolis: University of Minnesota Press, 1952.

Symphony News. The Newsletter of the American Symphony Orchestra League. Vienna, Virginia: The American Symphony Orchestra League, Vol. 24, No. 5 (October-November 1973).

Symphony News Is Good News. A publicity handbook for symphony orchestras and symphony women's associations. Vienna, Virginia, American Symphony Orchestra League, 1971.

Thompson, Helen M. *The Community Symphony Orchestra.* Charleston, West Virginia: The American Symphony Orchestra League, Inc., 1952.

Thompson, Helen M. *Report of Study on Governing Boards of Symphony Orchestras.* Charleston, West Virginia: The American Symphony Orchestra League, Inc., 1958.

Toffler, Alvin. *The Culture Consumers.* New York: St. Martin's Press, 1964.

United States Department of Treasury, Internal Revenue Service. Publications No. 526, "Income Tax Deduction for Contributions," issued annually, and No. 557, "How to Apply for Recognition of Exemption for an Organization," latest edition October 1977, summarize Internal Revenue Service policy regarding nonprofit organizations.

Walters, Michael J. "Aspects of Applied Instrumental Conducting." D.M.A. dissertation, University of Miami, 1971.

Wangerin, Richard H. Statement regarding proposals affecting tax treatment of Charitable Contributions to Tax-Exempt Organizations. Statement presented to the Committee on Ways and Means, United States House of Representatives, April 11, 1973. Vienna, Virginia: The American Symphony Orchestra League, Inc., 1973.

White, Leslie C., and Helen M. Thompson, eds. *Survey of Arts Councils.* Charleston, West Virginia: The American Symphony Orchestra League, Inc., 1959.

Woodbury, Ward. "Leadership in Orchestral Conducting." Ph.D. dissertation, University of Rochester, 1954.

Index

ABOUT THE AUTHOR

James Van Horn is concert coordinator at the University of Washington in Seattle and music director and conductor of the Bremerton, Washington, Symphony.